Mind Your King

Lessons and Essays on
Biblical Authority

Doy Moyer

Front cover art by Jennifer Watson
www.thearteest87.com

ISBN-10: 1530740487
ISBN-13: 978-1530740482

Contents

Part 1: Lessons

Part 2: Essays

Dedication

To my parents and in-laws who fought hard for the Lord's cause and sought to remain true to God's word in their generation.

My mother, *Patsy,* and my late father, *Forrest,* my parents who first introduced me to God and His word

Wayne and Peni Teel, my gracious in-laws whose commitment to the Lord has so strongly impacted generations after them

How lovely on the mountains
Are the feet of him who brings good news,
Who announces peace
And brings good news of happiness,
Who announces salvation,
And says to Zion, "Your God reigns!"

Isaiah 52:7

Introduction

To understand authority requires that we fully acknowledge the Lordship and Kingship of Jesus Christ. Jesus is the King. "Your God reigns!" is a key declaration of the gospel (Isa. 52:7). All authority is His (Matt. 28:18-20). If we respect this one aspect of Jesus, we will be ready and willing to respect His authority in all things.

"Why do you call Me, 'Lord, Lord' and do not do what I tell you?" (Luke 6:46) To call someone "Lord" shows respect for a person and his position. When it comes to Jesus, it is much more than a courtesy title. The connotations of calling Jesus "Lord" are great enough to completely change the course of one's life. The implications of the Lordship of Jesus require that a person bow in complete submission to Him and His will. When Thomas confessed Jesus, he called Him, "My Lord and my God" (John 20:28). Jesus is Lord in every way and over every aspect of life. He is King of Kings and Lord of Lords, with all rule, power, and dominion (Dan. 7:13-14; Rev. 19:16).

Christians ought to see the Lordship of Jesus in everything they do. It is at the foundation of the Christian's worldview, and there should not be anything that is untouched in a person's life, as if somehow the Christian can section off his or her life so that Jesus is not Lord over some aspect of it. Paul wrote, "Whatever you do, do your work heartily, as for the Lord rather than for men, knowing that from the Lord you will receive the reward of the inheritance. It is the Lord Christ whom you serve" (Col. 3:23-24).

The study of authority is not about developing a legalistic mindset, but it is about striving to glorify the Creator and honor His ways and thoughts. Our first and foremost desire is to honor and glorify God. With that in mind, we wish to make a few observations that are pertinent to this work.

First, we are approaching the study of authority from the position that Scripture is God's word and that Christians ought to be following it. We will not try to prove this point here, as that is beyond the scope of this material, but we will work from the assumption that it is the truth.

Second, this work is intended to consider and promote basic principles. It is not intended to answer every specific question that relates to authority, even if that were possible. No doubt some will wish more be said about this or that particular issue. However, the purpose is to understand the principles better so that the specifics can be discussed more intelligently and applications may be made more consistently. Many of the questions that relate to authority are best considered within a congregational context as each group weaves its way through various issues and difficulties. This work is by no means some kind of final say-so on every position and doctrine that is controversial. Don't look for lists of answers. Look for guiding principles that help improve the conversations and studies within a congregational setting. Use the principles to discuss other specifics not covered here. While we can write lessons on any number of topics that have implications concerning authority, it is more valuable in a congregational context to start with the principles, then have an intelligent discussion about the matter and determine proper applications within that setting. There should be sufficient examples of principles contained herein to help in looking at a number of other issues.

Third, this is about trying to understand the authority of God, as given through Scripture, by means of reasonable, common sense thinking. The issue really is not whether the New Testament is a "legal code." We aren't trying to create new laws. We are, however, trying to understand God's will. If God tells us something, and we recognize it to be applicable, we should willingly do it. If He shows us something, and we see how it applies and we can follow it, why would we not want to do it? All of Scripture, regardless of genre, is instruction and teaching, put there for a reason that we might learn what pleases and glorifies Him (cf. 2 Tim. 3:16-17). All of it is also here by God's grace. If we see what is revealed as all-encompassing for us, then we won't be so quick to separate out parts of our lives (our time vs. God's time), for every thought will be under the authority of and obedience to Christ. None of this changes the need to recognize context and to interpret properly, but it can change the attitude that we bring to the Scriptures as we read and study. I can only represent myself here. I realize not everyone will agree with my approach or all my conclusions, but I do ask for a fair hearing.

Ultimately, submitting to God's authority and grace is the essence of what it means to be His people. We cannot properly claim to be disciples of Jesus if we are refusing His authority. This authority is expressed in many ways. He is Lord. He is the King. He has all power. Since we are subjects of the King, then we ought to be concerned in how to understand His will for us. These lessons are intended to explore various principles that help with this process.

The book is divided into two parts. Part 1 is a series of thirteen lessons with questions that make it suitable for a class study. Part 2 contains several essays that touch on various issues that are often raised. May God bless us all as we strive to glorify Him by recognizing His divine power and rule over our lives, both individually and congregationally.

I want to especially thank my wife, Laurie, for her support, and my children and their families. They are my prime encouragement.

Caleb, Caitlin, and Eliana Moyer
Luke, Sarah, Joshua, Elizabeth, and Abigail Moyer
Audrey Moyer

Doy Moyer

Part 1

Lessons on Biblical Authority

The Meaning of Authority

Psalm 23/1/2 Jer. 17:9

Why must we consider authority in religion? What does that even mean? How do you think about authority? In order to set the stage for understanding the importance of recognizing God's authority as we serve Him, let's start with this important passage:

"How lovely on the mountains are the feet of him who brings good news, who announces peace and brings good news of happiness, who announces salvation, and says to Zion, 'Your God reigns!'" (Isa. 52:7).

This verse, quoted in Romans 10:15, contains one of the key messages of the gospel: God reigns! He is King. He is sovereign, and it is only through His exercise of sovereignty that we are saved. We, as His children of all people, should respect that Kingship. This is why authority matters: The Lord is king, and if we wish to take part in His salvation, we need to listen to Him. Authority, then, is grounded on at least these four pillars of truth:

First, God is the Creator (Gen. 1:1). As Creator, He has the right to tell us what to do and how to live.

Second, Jesus Christ is King (Acts 2:29-36). He sits on His throne and rules His kingdom. He is preeminent as the head over His body (Col. 1:18).

Third, the Holy Spirit is the Revealer of the mind of God (1 Cor. 2:10-13). The only way to know what God thinks is for Him to reveal His mind to us, and the Spirit has done this (2 Pet. 1:20-21).

Fourth, *mankind is God's creation, but is not in a position to be the authority* (Jer. 10:23). People are flawed sinners who cannot be the final standard of truth. We need God.

Authority as Fundamental

Consider the warning for those who have left the faith once for all delivered to the saints (Jude 3): "Woe to them! For they have gone the way of Cain, and for pay they have rushed headlong into the error of Balaam, and perished in the rebellion of Korah" (Jude 11).

What do these three situations share in common? At the heart of all three is an attitude that allows people to think that their way is better than God's, that their thoughts are higher than His, that their needs outweigh what God knows and plans for. These all paid the price for a spirit of rebellion against God's authority.

The way of Cain is a path to envy and hatred due to a failure to follow God's instructions by faith (Gen. 4).

The error of Balaam seeks to place worldly value and personal gain above God's will (Num. 22; cf. Num. 31:16; Deut. 23:4-5).

The rebellion of Korah was an effort to question the plan and order set in place by God for leading His people (Num. 16).

All sin is a rebellion against the nature and authority of God (1 John 3:4; Rom. 3:23). For example, Adam and Eve's sin in the garden was a result of distrusting God's authority in favor of their own (Gen. 3:5). They were listening to the wrong authority. Why would they, or anyone else, do this?

Do we need authority in our worship to God? Do we need God's permission to act on His behalf? Must we know that God approves of what we are doing? The answers may seem so obvious, but rebellion against the concept of authority is an old problem. History is filled with revolutions and rebellions against what is perceived as "bad authority." As Ramm wrote, "Protestation against authority is really against authority which is not authority in its own right, or authority which has become officious or excessive" (16). People rebel because they think there is a better path to follow.

The question of authority has touched the entire religious world; it is not just a problem among a small group of believers. J.I. Packer, in his *Fundamentalism and the Word of God*, noted, "The problem of authority is the most fundamental problem that the Christian Church ever faces. This is because Christianity is built on truth: that is to say, on the content of a divine revelation" (42). He argues the importance of having "the right criterion of truth, by which we may tell the word of God from human error.... We must expect to find error constantly assailing the truth; Christendom will always be a theological battlefield" (43). He writes that the "deepest cleavages in Christendom are doctrinal; and the deepest doctrinal cleavages are those which result from disagreement about authority. Radical divergences are only to be expected when there is no agreement as to the proper grounds for believing anything" (44). Problems over authority are not unique to only one body of people. All struggle with fundamental questions about the nature of authority.

First, authority is fundamental, as it lies at the heart of the most basic questions of doctrine and practice. Second, it is at the core of recognizing truth from error, as it concerns the source of truth itself. Third, it is a point of continual contention, as many divisions occur due to issues over authority. We must, therefore, reaffirm our faith and trust in God and His authority, seeking to teach future generations who will, in turn, face further issues relating to authority. The question of authority will never go away. What do you think happens when one generation ignores divine authority?

There is no getting around the fact that everyone follows someone's authority. In the absence of God's authority, we will make our own or follow another's. If we care about God's will, we will seek to minimize our own will, for we have no authority that can come from ourselves. "Not my will, but Yours be done" is the only justified attitude in the light of God's sovereignty (cf. Luke 22:42).

We know that we cannot be righteous in ourselves (Rom. 3:10). If this is so, then does it not also follow that we cannot be authoritative in ourselves about righteous matters? Seeking to establish our own authority is no different in principle from seeking to establish our own righteousness. We are wholly dependent upon God for both salvation and authority.

What do we mean by "authority"?

"Authority" is a loaded word with several meanings, so we need to define it. Generally, authority is the power to make and enforce laws, to command, determine, judge, or exact obedience. In these lessons, we are focusing on two basic aspects of authority:

First is the one who has authority based upon a held position. For example, a police officer has authority to enforce the law in a special way because of the position. A Judge has the right to pronounce judgments consistent with law. A king has the right to rule. Can you think of other positions that come with a level of authority? This is the power people have because of special roles. The ultimate authority that God possesses is based upon His position as the Creator. He has inherent authority, and the Bible establishes this from the first verse (Gen. 1:1). Remember, "Your God reigns!"

Second is delegated authority or permission given to another by one who has the power to grant it. We might think of having a license to act because we have been granted that power by a greater authority. This is the warrant we have to act. We might have a license to drive or permission to enter a guarded facility. Our permission, our license, is our authority.

When we say that we have God's authority, we are claiming that we have the permission from God to act. How that permission is discerned is an important study, but we start with the understanding that God is the ultimate source of authority. He determines the boundaries of permission. When we can safely know that God has permitted or authorized an action, then we can confidently say that we have the authority to do it.

Because of who God is (our Creator), any understanding of authority must flow from Him and His nature. He is our foundation. Included in this is Jesus Christ as Head and King, as well as His word, the sword of the Spirit (Eph. 6:17), as the standard of our faith and practice (John 12:48; 16:12-13).

Only God has the absolute right to rule, govern, command, and expect obedience. There is no deeper foundation, no one else on whom God must rely. He could rest upon none greater. He is the first and the last; there is no other God besides Him (Isa. 42:8). The position He occupies needs no further foundation.

God delegates all other authority. This includes the authority He gives to government (Rom. 13), to the home (Eph. 5), and to His church (Col. 1:18). No human individual or group of people has inherent authority in any ultimate sense. They only have it in the sense that they have been given permission by God to act in whatever capacity they work. This is our beginning point.

Conclusion

We need to respect God's authority. Since "God reigns," His kingship should be a fundamental part of our understanding about who He is and why His authority is so important. Then we need to understand what lies at the heart of all sin. Sin is essentially displacing God's authority for our own or another's. Let's learn to think through the different aspects of authority and seek to understand why the differences are significant.

Discussion Questions

1. How does Isaiah 52:7 help us understand that God's authority is tied to the message of the gospel? *"Your God reigns!"*

2. What attitudes did these men display, and why did their attitudes create so much trouble? *There way is better than Gods way.*

> A. Cain (Gen. 4):
> *envy and hatred failure to follow Gods instruction*
> B. Korah (Num. 16):
> *questioned Gods plan and the order set in place by God*
> C. Balaam (Num. 22; Num. 31:16; Deut. 23:4-5):
> *worldly value and personal gain above Gods will*

3. Why do people generally rebel against authority? Is such rebellion ever justified? *They think there is a better path   No*

4. Why is authority so fundamental to the Christian?
Because its based on truth, on the content of divine revelation

5. Why will the question of authority still exist even though we try to deny God's authority? *You be under a someones authority no matter the path you choose*

6. Why is the difference between inherent and delegated authority important to discern? *God is the beginning and end of authority. He can delegate it, but He is the authority*

7. When we say that we have authority to act, what kind of authority are we claiming, and why? *delegated because we have specific permission/instruction to act*

8. Why does God need no further foundation for authority other than Himself? *There is no one else for Him to rely his position needs no further foundation.*

Christic the King

Why is the kingship of God so important to us? We began with this great passage:

"How lovely on the mountains are the feet of him who brings good news, who announces peace and brings good news of happiness, who announces salvation, and says to Zion, 'Your God reigns!'" (Isa. 52:7).

(If you wish to consider more, please read also the following passages: Psalm 2; Psalm 110; Daniel 7:13-14; Matthew 2:2; 21:1-10; 27:11-14; 28:18-20; John 18:33-37; Acts 2:29-36; 13:20-37; Colossians 1:13; 1 Timothy 1:16-17; Revelation 19:11-16).

The implications of kingship for questions of authority are significant. If Jesus is King, then He has the final say in what He wants and how He ought to be pleased. The point here is to get the idea of the kingship of Jesus firmly grounded in our thinking.

Throughout the Hebrew Scriptures, God Promised a King.

The Old Testament narrative shows God's concern with bringing about a king through the seed of Abraham (Gen. 17:6, 16), Judah (Gen. 49:10), and David (2 Sam. 7:12-13). The prophets also looked forward to a Davidic King who would rule over His people (Isa. 9:6-7; Jer. 23:5; 30:9; 33:15; Ezek. 34:23; 37:24; Dan. 7:13-14; Hos. 3:5; Zech. 6:11-13) and the Psalms point to the Messiah as the promised King (Psalm 2; 110).

The New Testament Scriptures show that Jesus fulfills the promise of the Messiah and King. Matthew emphasizes Jesus' kingdom from His birth throughout (Matt. 2:2; 21:1-10; 27:11-14; 28:18-20), and the other gospel accounts agree (Mark 11:1-11; 12:35-37; 15:2; Luke

19:28-38; 23:1-5; John 18:33-37). In fact, kingdom emphasis in the gospels is directly related to Christ as the King (cf. Mark 1:14-15; Luke 17:20-21). Peter preached the kingship of Jesus on Pentecost (Acts 2:14-36), and Paul later preached the same (Acts 13:22-39). The epistles carry on the teaching (Phil. 2:9-11; Col. 1:13; 3:24; 1 Tim. 1:16-17), and Revelation emphasizes Jesus as King of kings and Lord of lords (19:11-16).

Jesus' Kingship Emphasizes His Authority.

We are not in a bilateral covenant with God where we are on equal terms with Him and get to have equal say in what we do. This is a unilateral covenant in which the Lord has complete and sole authority. Any and all permissions come from Him.

A king rules His kingdom. Dominion belongs to Him, and He is seated on the throne "far above all rule and authority and power and dominion, and every name that is named, not only in this age but also in the one to come." All things are "in subjection under His feet," and He is "head over all things to the church, which is His body, the fullness of Him who fills all in all" (Eph. 1:20-23). There is no limit to His authority.

As King, Jesus is Head of the body and has total preeminence (see Col. 1:15-18). He completely rules over His Kingdom. As Lord, He is our Master, our Owner. As Creator, He has the right to tell us what to do. For example, His command to "go teach" is based upon the fact that He has this authority (Matt. 28:18-20).

Authority begins with one who has the right to speak and expect others to listen. It is grounded in the idea that there is someone rightfully in charge and to which others are amenable. In Scripture, we already know that God is the ultimate Authority because He is the Creator of all. Yet one of the great terms that captures the heart of the concept of authority is that of King. To help understand the significance of the kingship of Jesus, let's consider Psalm 2.

A Brief Look at Psalm 2.

Psalm 2 is one of David's royal psalms. Imagine, after having become king (and even prior), how many enemies he would have had. The nations, in an uproar, devising evil, take their stand together against God and His anointed king in order to cast off the fetters of the king's (and God's) rule. God answers back through His own laughter, scoffing, and anger, but His answer is this: "I have installed My King upon Zion, My holy mountain" (vs. 6). God does not back off, but pushes forward His King who speaks on behalf of God.

God gave the decree: "You are My Son, today I have begotten You." This King is God's Son, and he would take the ends of the earth as His possession and rule with a rod of iron to shatter the nations like earthenware (vv 7-9). The warning has been given to the nations. They must respond with proper respect and worship or they will be judged and smashed. "Kiss the Son," they are told, or He will be angry and they will perish in their way (vv 10-12).

Notice how Psalm 2 picks up on the themes of Psalm 1. Psalm 1:1 and Psalm 2:12, nearly forming an *inclusio* (like bookends where a phrase is repeated for emphasis), speak of the blessed who come to God and take refuge in Him. The terms of 1:1 are repeated in Psalm 2, showing how the concept of the way of the wicked moves from individuals to a national level. The righteous man is the one who delights in God's Law and who will then speak God's decrees. Together, these two psalms show that the truly blessed are those who 1) submit to the rule of God, 2) love His word, and 3) refuse to take their stand with the wicked.

The implications should be plain enough: if we want to be blessed, we will submit to the rule of God. The rule or kingdom of God is paramount here. Two places in the New Testament will sufficiently demonstrate what Psalm 2 is talking about.

First, when Peter and John were threatened by the council, they went to their brethren and prayed (Acts 4:23-31). In the prayer, they referred back to Psalm 2:1-2. But now instead of applying the wicked mentality to the Gentiles, they apply it to the Jewish rulers who have rejected the rule of Jesus Christ. By rejecting Christ's rule, they have rejected God's rule; they have rejected the Kingdom of God. How ironic that Psalm 2 would come to be applied to the Jewish rulers who were supposed to be looking for the kingdom! They did indeed take their stand with wickedness in rejecting Jesus as King.

Second, Paul quotes from Psalm 2 in his sermon of Acts 13 (see vv. 32-39). The good news concerning God's promise to Abraham is fulfilled in Jesus "in that He raised up Jesus, as it is written in the second Psalm, 'You are My Son, today I have begotten You.' As for the fact that He raised Him from the dead..." "Begotten" here is not a reference to the origin or birth of Jesus. Jesus was not created. Neither is it speaking of His birth through Mary. Rather, this is a royal description of God bringing out His King as a proclamation of the reign of the anointed One. This is God showing His King to the world as a testament to His power and sovereignty. What event did this with such power? Look again at what Paul said. Jesus was of the physical lineage of David, but "declared the Son of God with power by the resurrection from the dead, according to the Spirit of holiness, Jesus Christ our Lord" (Rom. 1:3-4). Peter preached the same message, that Jesus was raised up and exalted to the right hand of God as both Lord and Christ (the anointed King, Acts 2:29-36).

God has made His love known through the death of Jesus (Rom. 5:8). God has made His rule known by raising Jesus from the dead. He had demonstrated His rule many times in other ways, but the resurrection is most powerful of all. Death is conquered through Jesus Christ! He reigns and rules over all the nations. And, as Psalm 2 indicates, the very ends of the earth (all people) are made aware of the rule of the Christ.

When we come face to face with the Kingship of Jesus, we are left with two options. We can go our own way, reject His rule, and be shattered in judgment, or we can "kiss the Son," submit to His rule, and find God's tremendous blessings.

Conclusion

There can be no submitting to Christ's rule without recognizing His authority over all that we do. As King, Jesus is the ruler. He is loving and gracious, but He still has absolute authority and dominion. To speak of His authority, then, is to speak of the power and dominion that belongs to Him. He has the right to command and expect obedience. Our task is to listen, fear Him, and obey. He is, to be sure, a benevolent King, but He also means business when it comes to our doing His will.

Discussion Questions

1. In the presentation of the gospel message, how important is the proclamation, "Your God reigns!"?

2. Why is the kingship of Jesus a vital doctrine in understanding biblical authority?

3. How did the Hebrew Scriptures point to a promised Davidic King?

4. Compare Peter's sermon in Acts 2:14-36 with Paul's sermon in Acts 13:22-39 with respect to the kingship of Jesus. How did they proclaim His kingship? What do they both say is the proof of this kingship?

5. What does it mean to recognize that we are not in a bi-lateral covenant with God, but rather a unilateral covenant? Why is this an important recognition?

6. Consider again Ephesians 1:20-23 and Colossians 1:15-18 (and their contexts). What do these passages have in common relative to the authority of Jesus, and what does this mean for His people?

7. What does Psalm 2 show about those who reject the kingship of the Son?

8. Why is submitting to the Son so vital to receiving the blessings from God?

The Example of Jesus

For a time, the question many were asking is, "What would Jesus do?" This can be an important question, if we recognize what Jesus did, in fact, do.

How does the example of Jesus help us understand the importance of following God's authority? "Your God reigns" is, again, one of the basic messages of the kingdom of God (Isa. 52:7). Christians need to know the foundation on which they are building their spiritual lives. This foundation is grounded in God Himself. Jesus is our king, and the Holy Spirit has given us an inspired message to follow. The message is more than just words on a printed page. The message—the word—is living and active, sharp and piercing, judging the thoughts and intentions of the heart (Heb. 4:12). Jesus, as the Word (John 1:1), provides for us a living example to follow in His steps. If we will understand biblical authority, then we need to be dedicated to Jesus and His example.

Following the Example of Jesus

In calling ourselves disciples of Christ, we are saying that we will follow Jesus. If the pattern of Jesus was to ensure His pleasing God in all things, then what should we do? Since Jesus is our example, then we need to ask a fundamental question: what was Jesus' attitude toward Scripture? Should we not, as His disciples, seek to have the same attitude toward Scripture that He showed?

Jesus' attitude is seen when, in His response to the temptations, He stated, "It is written…" (Luke 4; Matt. 4). In response to the first, he quoted from Deuteronomy 8: "Man shall not live on bread alone, but on every word that proceeds out of the mouth of God." Moses had recounted Israel's time in the wilderness, where the test was whether or not they would keep God's commandments. They failed, but Jesus succeeded. Note here that there is complete recognition on Jesus' part that God's word must be the determining factor in following God. Man lives on what God says. If we care about eternal life, we will care deeply about God's word.

Further, Jesus taught, "It is the Spirit who gives life; the flesh profits nothing; the words that I have spoken to you are spirit and are life" (John 6:63). The situation prompted Peter to say, "Lord, to whom shall we go? You have words of eternal life" (vs. 68). Jesus saw that what was "written" as God's word had the authority of God stamped on it. He viewed the Scriptures as having God's authority. What Scripture says, God says. Do we follow Him in this attitude?

The next question is as important: what was Jesus' attitude toward respecting God's commands? That Jesus never sinned (Heb. 4:15-16; 2 Cor. 5:21) and never took the liberty to do whatever He wanted apart from the Father's will speaks volumes. He said, "My food is to do the will of Him who sent Me and to accomplish His work" (John 4:34). He also stated, "As I hear, I judge; and My judgment is just, because I do not seek My own will, but the will of Him who sent Me" (John 5:30). Since Jesus dedicated Himself completely to do God's will, and never took on His own initiative apart from the Father's will, then should we not seek to follow His example in this? If we are self-seeking, we are not following Christ. Breaching God's authority is a result of not seeking His will before ours, and of taking our own initiative apart from what God has revealed. In doing this, we are not following the example of Jesus, and therefore are not acting as His disciples.

Jesus never distinguished between His authority and the authority of written Scripture. To follow Jesus is to listen to His word (see John 12:48; Heb. 1:1-3). What will true disciples of Christ seek to do (John 8:31)? What kind of attitude toward Scripture and God's commands will they seek to have (1 Pet. 5:5; Jas. 4:6-8; Phil. 2:5)?

Whose Will am I Seeking?

Everyone listens to some authority, whether self-generated or from others. Rejection of authority isn't rejection of all authority whatsoever; it is trading one authority for another, and trading one pattern for another. This is why we need constant reminding that the essence of the gospel is to proclaim, "Your God reigns!" (Isa. 52:7) This is the foundation for the announcement of peace, good news of happiness, and salvation. Christ is King.

The kingdom is about God's rule. It is about His will being done "on earth as it is in heaven" (Matt. 6:10). This is at the heart of authority. To say that we don't need authority is to say that we don't really need the rule of the King. To emphasize the kingdom is to emphasize that God rules and has all authority. We cannot preach the kingdom and not preach the rule of the King. Further, God's authority and God's will are inseparable. To say, "Not as I will, but as You will" (Matt. 26:39), is to bow to His authority. Again, if this was Jesus' attitude on earth, how much more should it be ours—we who are not God and do not have any inherent authority on our own? If God's will is important to us at all, then we want to know how He communicates that will to us.

Knowing God's will is vital, particularly since our attitude should be to please God in all that we do. Read carefully the following passages with these two questions in mind: 1) What is the common idea in these passages?, and 2) How do these passages inform us about the kind of attitude we ought to have toward God's will?

- "Jesus said to them, 'My food is to do the will of Him who sent Me and to accomplish His work'" (John 4:34).
- "I can do nothing on My own initiative. As I hear, I judge; and My judgment is just, because I do not seek My own will, but the will of Him who sent Me" (John 5:30).
- "... I always do the things that are pleasing to Him" (John 8:29).

- "Not everyone who says to Me, 'Lord, Lord,' will enter the kingdom of heaven, but he who does the will of My Father who is in heaven will enter" (Matt. 7:21).
- "And without faith it is impossible to please Him, for he who comes to God must believe that He is and that He is a rewarder of those who seek Him" (Heb. 11:6).
- "...and those who are in the flesh cannot please God" (Rom. 8:8).
- "For the flesh sets its desire against the Spirit, and the Spirit against the flesh; for these are in opposition to one another, so that you may not do the things that you please" (Gal. 5:17).
- "Therefore we also have as our ambition, whether at home or absent, to be pleasing to Him" (2 Cor. 5:9).
- "No soldier in active service entangles himself in the affairs of everyday life, so that he may please the one who enlisted him as a soldier" (2 Tim. 2:4).
- "So that you will walk in a manner worthy of the Lord, to please Him in all respects" (Col. 1:10).
- "Whatever you do, do your work heartily, as for the Lord rather than for men, knowing that from the Lord you will receive the reward of the inheritance. It is the Lord Christ whom you serve" (Col. 3:23-24).

Think again about the message of these passages, for they give us one of the keys to understanding authority issues. The question is simply this: am I wanting to do God's will or my own? Authority issues are about attitudes. Are we trying to please ourselves or God? Are we enthroning ourselves as kings or do we submit to His rule as King? If I deny self, then it will never be about what I want, what feels good to me, what sounds good to me, or what satisfies me in the area of good works. It will be about what God wants as expressed by Him in His revelation. If that's not what it's about, then I haven't denied myself. I have merely used God's name as a rubber stamp upon my will.

When confronted with a question about authority and practice, is our reaction to think something like, "I would never accept that," or "There's no way I would believe that," or "But it's what I want to do anyway," instead of asking, "What does the Lord desire?" If so, then we are showing that we think our will is more important than God's. We must not decide practice and belief based on our desires. Instead, we must be ready to accept the Lord's will, no matter how disagreeable or different it may be from our will. Perhaps one of the reasons we struggle so much with God's authority is that we don't like to be told what to do. Even in admitting to God's authority, if we aren't careful, we may still be doing what we want under the guise of calling it God's will. Self-will can be quite deceptive that way. Yet God's authority is all-encompassing. We either accept it in humility, regardless of the consequences for our desires, or we forego it in favor of our desires. Commitment to Jesus Christ is, necessarily, a commitment to His authority wherein we seek His will and not our own.

Conclusion

Are we seeking to follow the example of Jesus in His respect for Scripture? Are we seeking God's will or ours? When we answer these questions, we will know a great deal about our view of biblical discipleship. How are we doing in following the example and will of Jesus Christ?

Discussion Questions

1. What does it mean to be disciples of Jesus?

We will follow Jesus

2. How should discipleship be shown in our approach to Scripture?

we should have the same attitude as Jesus

3. How did Jesus respond to His temptations, and why is this important for understanding His view of Scripture?

It is written. He recognizes its power and authority

4. How is the word of God tied to eternal life?

Gods word is the determine factor in following God

5. Why should we keep "Your God reigns" before us as we think about authority? *Because he reigns always. not back Then. He reigns Now and forever*

6. How does pleasing God contrast with being "in the flesh" in the cited passages? *"in the flesh" is pleasing me, not God*

7. In what ways are authority issues about attitudes?

we try to have equal say like we are on Gods level

8. Why do we sometimes struggle with authority?

Selfishness. Its hard to think what does the Lord desire. We Think what do we desire.

The Need for Authority

Since God reigns (Isa. 52:7), and because the Scriptures are the word of God, they are authoritative for what we are to believe and practice (2 Tim. 3:16-17). Man alone is incapable of being a trustworthy source of authority for others (Prov. 14:12; Jer. 10:23). Only Scripture, as God's word, can fill the need as our source of faith and authority (Rom. 10:17; Jude 3; 1 Pet. 4:11; Heb. 4:12-13).

God, as Creator, has the right to tell us what to do and how to think (Gen. 1:1). Man has no right to ignore this. We are under God's authority because He reigns (Isa. 52:7). Jesus Christ, as the Creator, is in a position of full authority over us, and we must submit to His will (Matt. 28:18; John 1:1-5; Col. 1:15-18; Luke 6:46; John 12:48).

How does Scripture show us our deep need for God's rule in our lives? Scripture doesn't just tell us to be under God's authority, it shows us through the many examples and passages that speak to the need. Here we will consider a few of these examples and some significant lessons they teach us.

This Need For Authority Is Illustrated In The Old Testament.

Examples, both good and bad, are given to us so that we may learn vital lessons about how to serve God. They are for our instruction and can provide hope (Rom. 15:4). They can also serve as warnings against taking an evil path and having to deal with undesirable consequences (1 Cor. 10:1-13). Several examples in the Old Testament show us that mankind needs to follow the authority of God. Consider the following illustrations of this need:

Adam and Eve (Gen. 3:1-6). Their problem was a failure to submit to God's authority. They listened to the lie that they did not need to submit to God's authority, but could establish their own (Gen. 3:5). They could decide for themselves what was right and wrong. They didn't need God telling them what to do. This is the lie of secular humanism and is still prominent today. It undermines the authority of God and makes light of His severity.

Cain and Abel (Gen. 4). Abel's sacrifice was accepted because he acted by faith. This means he listened to God and did what God said, since faith comes by hearing God's word (Heb. 11:4; Rom. 10:17). Abel's is an example that provides hope. Cain's sacrifice, on the other hand, was refused because he did not act by faith. He acted presumptuously and substituted his own will for God's.

Nadab and Abihu (Lev. 10:1-3). They offered up "strange fire" which the Lord "had not commanded them." God had told His priests what He wanted, and these priests substituted their will for God's. Because of their insolence against God's authority, and their failure to honor Him, they were punished severely.

Korah's rebellion (Num. 16). God had chosen the family of Aaron to be priests. Korah questioned God's authority and presumed that he and others could also serve as priests, even though they were not told they could. They rebelled against God's appointed leader, Moses, and incurred the wrath of God. This would have been unnecessary had he listened to God in the first place (vv. 3, 9).

Moses' failure (Num. 20:1-13). While much of what Moses did provides a good example that gives hope, here Moses and Aaron rebelled against God's authority. God's assessment was that Moses did not believe Him or treat Him as holy. As a consequence, Moses was unable to enter the Promised Land.

The New Cart (1 Chron. 13:1-12; 15:12-15). God specified that the ark of the covenant was to be carried by the Levites, but they tried to move it by using a new cart. Perhaps they thought their way was more expedient. It appears that they had good intentions. Even if Uzza had good intentions in trying to keep the ark from falling, they still disobeyed God. They "did not seek Him according to the ordinance" (15:13). They failed to consult God on the matter and presumed their way would be fine. By doing this they violated the authority of God. Is it possible that we might do the same today?

King Uzziah entering the temple (2 Chron. 26:16-20). Burning incense was a good work, ordained by God. However, it was given to the priests. Uzziah tried to enter the temple to burn incense, and he sinned because of his pride. He was told, "it is not for you, Uzziah..." (vs. 18). Uzziah was acting upon his own authority, to which he was not entitled, even as king. God desires for things to be done His way. Should we also learn to be content with His ways?

More examples can be cited. We might think of Noah (Gen. 6), Saul (1 Sam. 15), and Jeroboam (1 Kings 12:25-33). Can you think of more? What lessons do you take from these? What are we shown through these examples, and why are they there? All of this should help impress us with the need to listen to the authority of God. Through these illustrations, we are shown the need to do what God says and refrain from presumption (cf. Deut. 4:1-6; Prov. 30:6).

This Need For Authority Is Illustrated In The New Testament.

The New Testament also shows the need to abide by God's authority. The Pharisees questioned Jesus (Matt. 21:23-27): "By what authority are You doing these things, and who gave You this authority?" The question recognizes first, that there is a need for authority, and second, that the authority must come from One who has the power to grant it. If it comes from one who doesn't have such power, it is useless.

Jesus responded by pointing out that there are only two possible sources of authority: Heaven (i.e., God) or men. Now the only way that one can know whether or not something comes from God is by looking into His will. If it cannot be found in His will, then it is authored by men. What other choices are there? If we want to please God, then how important is it that we make sure that what we do is authored by God?

Remember Jesus' view of God's will and our need to follow. Think again about Matthew 7:21-23: "Not everyone who says to Me, 'Lord, Lord,' will enter the kingdom of heaven; but he who does the will of My Father who is in heaven. Many will say to Me on that day, 'Lord, Lord, did we not prophesy in Your name, and in Your name cast out demons, and in Your name perform many miracles?' And then I will declare to them, 'I never knew you; depart from Me, you who practice lawlessness.'" What is lawlessness? Are we okay simply because we attach the name of Jesus to something?

Many other passages demonstrate this need (Luke 6:46; John 8:31-32; 1 Cor. 4:6; Phil. 3:16; Eph. 6:1-6; Col. 3:17; 2 Thess. 2:7; Heb. 5:9; 1 Pet. 4:11; 2 John 9-11; Rev. 22:18-19). Take time to read and study these. The New Testament shows that God will not approve substituting our own will for His.

Everyone listens to some authority. If we deny the need for God's, then we will look to ourselves or to others as authority. At some point, we have to ask that question, "How's that working for you?" There is no getting around it. Can we afford to reject the authority of God in favor of our own (Prov. 14:12; Matt. 15:9; Col. 2:20-22)? This is why we must continue to plead for teaching that is rooted in Scripture (cf. Isa. 8:20; 1 Pet. 4:11). Failure to recognize and submit to the authority of God will result in our own loss (Matt. 7:21-23).

Conclusion

We know that good intentions do not make a wrong action right. We must consult God and His word about the proper ways in which we are to serve Him. Presumption and pride result in a rejection of the authority which God possesses. Instead, we must respect His authority by humble submission to His will as recorded in the Scriptures.

Discussion Questions

1. Why are examples from the Old Testament important to us today? *given for our benefit. given for our advisement, for our instruction*

2. How do each of the given examples from the Old Testament warn us against ignoring God's authority? *Becoming wise in our own eyes leads to our destruction.*

3. Besides the ones given, what are some other examples that you can think of? How do they show the need to listen to God's authority? *Ananias & Sapphire lying to God. Not giving what they said.*

4. Discuss the account of Matthew 21:23-27. How does the question from the Pharisees illustrate the sources of authority? How does Jesus' response solidify the point? *There is a need for authority. It must come from the One true Source together. It is not from Men it must be from heaven*

5. What is Jesus' view of the will of God, according to Matthew 7:21-23? What should our attitude be about the will of God? *we must live for God. Not simply call on him we when we need them*

6. What is lawlessness and why is it so destructive in our relationship with God? *If dont follow his law we have no relationship with him*

7. Collectively, what do the passages from this lesson show us with respect to how we should treat God's will? *We should respect and believe it is God breathed authority. It should not be questioned*

8. How is it true that everyone listens to some authority, even when people deny God's authority? *We are following some authority whether its ours or someone elses*

Do We Really Need Authority?

Do we really need authority (permission from God) in all that we do in our service toward Him? Some may think not, but once the negative position is taken, it traps the person in a nebulous, subjective thought-process of being more concerned about what mankind thinks rather than what God thinks. If our goal is to please God, then we cannot afford to deny the need for authority from Him. The question then is, to borrow from Paul, "For am I now seeking the favor of men, or of God? Or am I striving to please men? If I were still trying to please men, I would not be a bond-servant of Christ" (Gal. 1:10). That which pleases God (or displeases Him) is what the subject of authority is all about. If we make it our aim to please Him in all things (cf. 2 Cor. 5:9), then we are necessarily making it our goal to follow His authority in all things. These ideas cannot be separated. If we decide to act without God's authority, then we are deciding against trying to serve and please Him in favor of pleasing ourselves.
— Doy Moyer (excerpt from Authority in Worship, 2005 Florida College Lectures)

Knowing What God Wants

Essay 9 (handwritten)

God reigns (Isa. 52:7), and this means we need to be concerned about God's will. This also means that we must be concerned with *knowing what* God wants and *knowing how* God communicates His will. Remember that the Holy Spirit is the Revealer of God's mind (1 Cor. 2:13), so we must pay attention to what the Spirit has revealed. Here we are asking how basic communication works because this will inform us about how God communicates with us. What we are talking about here is typical of all communication. If you want to communicate your will to someone, how will you do it? If God communicates His will to us, how does He do it? There is no magical formula here. However communication occurs is how anyone's will is made known, and God has communicated to us in the very same ways we would try to communicate to others, whether we are parents, workers, employers, and in all other avenues of life. All we are doing here is recognizing, in a logical and reasonable way, that God communicates His will to us in the same way. If we are going to understand God's authority, we should step back and consider how this happens.

It's How Communication Works.

There are some basic premises in understanding how God communicates His will or authority. God communicates His will in the same ways we communicate our wills. By understanding how we fundamentally communicate, we will understand more about how God communicates.

People may buck against the idea of "establishing" authority from God, but the issue is simply how God communicates His will. When we know that, we've answered how His authority is made known. How is anyone's will communicated? If you are going to communicate what you want, how will you do it? This gets to the heart of the issue. Really, there are three basic ways to communicate something:

First, we tell others what we want. This is direct and can be an order or statement.

Second, we show others what we want and how to do it. Illustrations, examples, or models are part of this process.

Third, we imply what we expect others to get by what we say or show. This can even be done through gestures or silence, depending on the context. When people "get it," then they have inferred from the implication what we wanted them to get. For example, a principle might come from what we are told, and we may infer from the stated principle a proper application to our current situation.

Any attempt at communication will utilize at least one of these. Try to communicate without them! If others disagree just ask them to express that disagreement without telling, showing, or implying anything about it. Telling, showing, and implying are logically self-evident. No further proof is needed, as objections to this are self-defeating and logically incoherent.

Does this kind of communication come from God or man? Our abilities to think logically and communicate do come from God. He made us creatures with the need and ability to communicate, and this is just how it is done. To help us understand God's authority, then, we need to start with the logical premises and show that there is no way around how communication works. We are simply reminding people of the fundamental logic that underlies all communication, including God's.

The process of telling, showing, and implying is not itself a method of interpretation. Rather, it is a recognition of how we get the raw data that then is interpreted. In other words, we start with the facts: what did God say? What has been shown? Then we proceed to interpret these.

Tell, Show, and Imply in Action: Acts 10

We have argued that communication, in its most basic form, takes place through the process of telling, showing, and implying. No one can communicate without doing at least one of these in some form. This is what the communicator brings to the process. The receptor, on the other hand, takes what is told, shown, or implied and interprets that material. The receptor is asking, "What do these mean? How do they apply to my situation?"

Scripture gives multiple and varied examples of these forms of communication as they express God's will. We are going to focus here on how God communicated His will to Peter in Acts 10. As a Jew, Peter had grown up learning not to associate with gentiles (vs. 28). This is understandable, given that God was clear about His people not mixing with the pagan nations. All of this was about to change, and this change illustrates the process of telling, showing, and implying. It is also the way that Peter knew God's will about preaching to the gentiles.

First, God showed Peter a vision that was intended to teach something vital about God's intentions. Peter had gone up on a housetop to pray, but fell into a trance in which he saw this vision of an object like a sheet lowered down by the four corners (vv. 9-16). In this sheet were four-footed animals, creatures, and birds. Then a voice told him to get up, kill these creatures, and eat. Peter refused, saying that he had never eaten anything unholy or unclean. The voice responded, "What God has cleansed, no longer consider unholy." This happened three times. Peter was shown something by God, and he recognized this, as he indicates in vs. 28: "God has *shown* me…"

Second, God directly told Peter to go with the gentiles who were coming to ask for him. After the vision, while Peter was contemplating what it meant, three men showed up looking for him. Before, Peter might have tried to avoid this circumstance. However, the Spirit told him, "get up, go downstairs and accompany them without misgivings, for I have sent them Myself" (vs. 20). Peter was told to go, so he did.

Third, Peter inferred that he should not call any man common or unclean. Peter had to think about what that vision meant, coupled with the fact that God told him to go with those men to the gentiles. He figured it out, as his words to Cornelius demonstrate: "You yourselves know how unlawful it is for a man who is a Jew to associate with a foreigner or to visit him; and yet God has shown me that I should not call any man unholy or unclean. That is why I came without even raising any objection when I was sent for. So I ask for what reason you have sent for me?"

Peter drew a required conclusion based on what he had been shown and told. The context helped to make it obvious. Yet there is nowhere in the text where God says, "The gentiles are now clean and you may preach to them." Perhaps Peter could have reasoned that the vision was only about animals and food, not men. Nowhere in the vision is there anything about men. Perhaps he could have concluded that God wanted him to go with those men for some other reasons. Those gentiles were the ones who said that Cornelius wanted to hear a message from him. How did he know they weren't lying? How could he trust them? He had to trust what he was told, and he inferred that what God showed him was really about men.

Peter put all the pieces together. The vision showed him something about clean and unclean. The Spirit told him to go with them and that this was all from God. He trusted the Spirit and the context. When he arrived, he realized the implications of what he was told and shown. He was not to call any man common or unclean.

Through telling, showing, and implying, God communicated His will to Peter. "But wait a minute," one might object. "The purpose of this passage isn't to explain how God communicates His authority." No, God's purpose was to communicate something to Peter, who, in turn, would communicate the gospel to Cornelius and his family. This would then show that the gentiles were proper recipients of the gospel. All we are doing is paying attention to how this happened. We are seeing the ways in which God communicated His will to others. We are not creating a new form of interpretation; we are observing and making an application.

The situation in Acts 10 shows us that God values the entire communication process. He could have told Peter explicitly not to call any man unclean, without giving him a vision. He could have spelled it out completely for Peter. Instead, God chose to show him something, tell him something, and imply something that he expected Peter to understand by putting all the information together. God values the process that includes implication and inference. He values the ability He has given to us to reason things out and draw warranted conclusions. He wants his people to think through the implications of what is told and shown in the expression of His will. This is "tell, show, and imply" in action. If God valued that process, so should we.

Conclusion

The communication process is straightforward in principle. There are only so many ways to try to communicate, and these will always entail some form of telling, showing, and implying. There is just no other way to do it. Our argument is that God has communicated to us in these very ways. He tells us what He wants, shows us what He wants, and implies what He expects us to get. This is not some special method of interpretation, but rather a process by which we, as the receivers, recognize the data given to us by God.

Discussion Questions

1. How does communication work? Why would we say that "tell, show, and imply" are the primary ways?

2. How does understanding the fundamental communication process help us understand God's authority?

3. How would you respond to the question, "Does the communication process come from God or man?" Why?

4. Why would we say that "tell, show, and imply" is not itself a method of interpretation? How does the process give us the raw data?

5. How did the vision given to Peter, in Acts 10, show him that he should not call any man common or unclean?

6. Why did the Spirit tell Peter to go without any misgivings? Why would Peter have had misgivings?

7. What relevant information did Peter have in order to infer what he did about preaching to the gentiles? What reasoning process would cause one to conclude what Peter did?

8. Why would we say that God valued the "tell, show, and imply" process? Why should we value the process?

Implication and Inference

One of the more difficult issues in understanding communication, including authority, is that of inference. Some have become so disenchanted with the abuses of inference that they have just about given up on it as a reliable way to understand anything. This, however, is an over-reaction that is both unwarranted and impossible to bear out consistently. The reason is that inference is a necessary part of reasoning. No one can avoid inferences. The question is whether or not the inferences are warranted, legitimate, and reasonable. They must not be contrived or forced.

The definition of inference is: "in logic, derivation of conclusions from given information or premises by any acceptable form of reasoning. Inferences are commonly drawn (1) by deduction, which, by analyzing valid argument forms, draws out the conclusions implicit in their premises, (2) by induction, which argues from many instances to a general statement, (3) by probability, which passes from frequencies within a known domain to conclusions of stated likelihood, and (4) by statistical reasoning, which concludes that, on the average, a certain percentage of a set of entities will satisfy the stated conditions" (*Encyclopaedia Britannica* online).

The communicator implies and the receiver infers. To imply is to indicate something without explicitly stating it. To infer is to get what is being implied. There are many things that affect how we infer something, but that we infer is a fact of reasoning. Richard Paul and Linda Elder state in their *Miniature Guide to Critical Thinking*, "All reasoning contains inferences or interpretations by which we draw conclusions and give meaning to data."

No reasoning takes place without drawing conclusions (inferring) from implications. Statements and examples usually come with the expectation that we draw further conclusions (the statements and examples are the data that we must infer from and to which we give meaning). The point of reasoning and discerning is that we are capable of taking what is given whether implicitly or explicitly, then reasoning to proper conclusions.

Implications can be both powerful and binding.

Some ask, "Are inferences binding?" They are wondering if what we infer can be required. When the communicator (in this case, God) implies something, and He expects us to infer or interpret His implication properly (that is, we are to "get it"), then yes it can be a required conclusion. Think back to Acts 10 and God's expectation that Peter infer properly that gentiles should not be considered unclean. That inference was required. Some implications are binding and some aren't, and we need to pay attention to the context of the passage. In order to better understand the principle, let's consider some examples demonstrating that every Christian believes in the binding power of an implication.

First, anyone who is a Christian today has accepted, by inference, that people of all places and times ought to be Christians. There is no direct statement telling us explicitly that 21st century Americans should be Christians. We infer that Christianity was intended to be taken beyond the boundaries of the first century time-frame. This inference is necessary. Otherwise, on what basis should anyone be a Christian today (see Matt. 28:18-20; Acts 17:30-31)?

Second, when we follow particular commands in Scripture, we do so because we have inferred that those commands are viable for those beyond the original audience. That these commands are required is evident, but if we believe we should be following particular commands that were given to the Roman, Corinthian, or Colossian Christians, then we do so on the basis of what is implied by Scripture and what we infer as readers. Are these inferences necessary? We believe so.

Some matters of right and wrong must be inferred. Paul ends his list of sins in Galatians 5:19-21 with "things like these." How can we know what this means? The Hebrews writer speaks of the mature who can "discern good and evil" (Heb. 5:12-14). Discerning requires inferring from known principles.

Here is a case in point to help clarify how we believe that inferences are required. What is the greatest commandment given? Jesus explicitly said that the greatest commandment is to love God with all your heart, soul, strength, and mind (Matt. 22:34-40; Mark 12:28-34). If we believe this is still the greatest commandment, then on what basis do we believe it? We ask this because it illustrates the power of an implication.

In context, Jesus was speaking about the Law and the Prophets. He said nothing explicitly about the New Covenant in this context. If the command is to be understood beyond the Hebrew Scriptures, then we are inferring its necessity beyond the original context.

Further, this command is not explicitly stated this way elsewhere in the New Testament. There are plenty of passages telling us to love one another. We know that we need to love God. However, where are we explicitly told elsewhere that loving God with all the heart, soul, strength, and mind is the *greatest* commandment? The only place that is found is in a passage that contextually is speaking of the Law and the Prophets. We infer the rest.

Even in the Hebrew Scriptures, where does it say that loving God with all the heart, soul, strength, and mind is the *greatest* of the commandments? The command is there (Deut. 6:4), but how were they to know it was the greatest? If they were expected to know it, then they knew it by what is implied. Some did get it. For example, the lawyer who asked Jesus about inheriting eternal life answered the question correctly (Luke 10:25-29). How did he know that inheriting eternal life was so connected to loving God with all the heart? That is not stated in Deuteronomy 6. Where does that passage say anything about "eternal life"? Yet, Jesus said that the lawyer answered his own question correctly. That must have been a pretty significant inference. Was it binding?

Do we believe in the power of an implication? If we are Christians, and we believe that loving God with all your heart is still the greatest commandment, then we believe in the power of implication. The question is not whether implications and inferences are part of our biblical understanding. They are vital for every reader. The question is whether we are inferring properly.

On Principle and Inference

A principle is a fundamental truth from which other laws or behaviors are derived. Upon understanding a principle, we recognize various applications that come from it. For example, based on the principle of treating others as we want to be treated (Matt. 7:12), we might infer that we should mow the lawn of a needy neighbor. The applications might be unstated and we must infer the specifics. Principles are accepted and applied through the process of inferring from the data we are given. If we believe in principles, then we accept implications and inferences.

Inferences are taken to task by those who question whether or not they are adequate for understanding anything authoritative. They may then speak of principles guiding their behavior. In truth, there is no living by principle if inferences have no power, for proper applications will involve inferences. Otherwise, principles would be empty ideas with no real-world application. Here is the argument: 1) everyone uses applied principles; 2) applying principles requires inference; 3) therefore, everyone uses inference.

Many explicit precepts also require us to work through proper applications. For example, we are told, "love your enemies, and do good, and lend, expecting nothing in return; and your reward will be great, and you will be sons of the Most High; for He Himself is kind to ungrateful and evil men. Be merciful, just as your Father is merciful" (Luke 6:35-36). Yet how is all of this to be carried out? We can define love and mercy the way we wish (subjective and self-willed), or we can dig further into Scripture and see how God showed love and mercy. Then, we can see how to make applications in our own time. All of this requires inferring from then to now and from God's actions to ours. Without inference, there is no modern application.

These are self-evident principles of authority. What God has told us, shown us, and implied are on every page. We cannot rightly say, "Only commands are binding," for even then we will have crippled our abilities to make modern applications of those commands. If we cannot infer, then we cannot apply. We recognize that inferences can be unnecessary and lead to an abuse of a text. However, the fact that an abuse can take place does not invalidate the point. Rather, it drives home the need to be careful in drawing conclusions and making applications. The interpretation of Scripture needs to be attended by good reason and a great care for context. That is why this particular subject is important. If we care about principle, we'll care about proper reasoning from the principle to the applications.

Conclusion

Implications and inferences are an integral part of the communication process. We are forced to use our minds to think things out and through. There are dangers, however, and we must be careful that we are using our reasoning process properly so that we are not forcing conclusions where they are not warranted. When warranted, however, the power of inferences is self-evident. Let us learn to use them appropriately.

Discussion Questions

1. What are implications and inferences? How do we imply?
Instructions given with given the specific direction.

2. Why would we say that implications and inferences are a necessary part of the communication process?
We infer everyday. You logically deduct and apply into to make decisions

3. How can implications from 2,000 years ago be binding today?
They are directed by God to all christians at all times not just 2000 yrs ago.

4. On what basis do we follow any command that is given in Scripture? *Is instruction from God*

5. How does the command to love God with all the heart illustrate the binding power of an implication? *It was directed at we have to infer its power beyond the Hebrew Scripture*

6. What is a principle, and what role do principles play in our understanding of Scripture? *fundamental truth from which other laws and behaviors are derived*

7. Why would we argue that inferences are necessary for applying principles? *They are accepted as good through the process of inferring*

8. Why should we be cautious with the inferences we make?

We cant make an inference in places they were meant to be made.
We shouldnt force conclusion were they are not warranted.

Examples

Since God reigns (Isa. 52:7), we are concerned with the examples God provides in His revelation. When we build something, we often look at patterns or models. We like to see examples of what something should look like. Examples give us a model or picture, showing us what God likes or doesn't like. In our efforts to be conformed to the image of Christ, we need to pay special attention to the Exemplar, Jesus Christ, and to what He authorizes through His chosen apostles (see 1 Cor. 11:1; Phil. 3:17). While much can be said about the nature of examples, let's consider some basic principles and check our attitudes about examples.

Basics on Examples

Some ask, "When is an example binding?" That may be the wrong question to start with. Let's ask, "What is God intending to show us?" Instead of a list of "rules," let's think about these principles:

Without any indication from God (general or specific), we should not presume to know God's will. His silence is not an open invitation to do whatever we wish. A positive example shows that God approves of something; He is not silent. He has shown what He likes and we should try to follow it if possible. The fact that He has shown us something means that we may then act in that same way, insofar as we are able, with God's approval. However, if there is no further information given about that issue, then we should act based on what He has shown rather than what He has not shown. The question is, what does the example show us to do or not do?

Examples illustrate how we may act with God's approval, and those examples give us freedom to so act. For instance, God shows approval, through an example, of His disciples coming together on the first day of the week to partake of the Lord's supper (Acts 20:7). By following this example, we can know God is pleased. In this way, God shows us what He wants by giving examples of how to please Him. How do we know we are on the right track here? First, because the Lord tells us that we are to consider what the apostles show us through their examples (Phil. 3:17; 4:9). Second, if the apostles were acting upon the authority of God, then what they do by God's approval is significant. They spoke by God's authority, and we are told to listen to them as we would Christ (John 13:20; John 16:13; Gal. 4:14; 1 Cor. 14:37).

We may not have all recorded statements of what God said, but when an action was done with God's approval through the apostles, then God already authorized it. They weren't just making things up as they go. When we imitate what we are shown, we know we are acting upon God's authority because positive examples illustrate actions that are permitted and desired by God.

Simplifying Examples

We are to love God with all our heart, soul, strength, and mind (Mark 12:30). When we see examples of God's people doing what pleases Him, should we not desire to follow their examples? If we ask, "But is that example binding?" aren't we really asking, "Do we have to?" Wouldn't those who love God want to follow an example that God saw fit to show us? Let's ask instead, "What does this show us about what God desires?" By God's grace we have an example of something that He likes. The Scriptures aren't huge, so when an example shows God's approval, wouldn't those who love Him want to take special note? If we are able, and if our circumstances are comparable, wouldn't we want to follow what God, in His grace, found important enough to include in His message?

Which God-pleasing example would we *not* want to follow? Is there a specific case of His disciples acting with His approval that we would look at and say, "No, we don't want to do that"? If we are able, and our situation is comparable, should we look at something that pleases Him, argue it is not necessary, then ignore it? What should be our attitude toward such examples?

Are there details in examples that are not necessary? We recognize, in normal communication, that not every detail is as significant as another. For instance, if I show someone how I want a task to be accomplished on a computer, and in the process of this I sit in a chair with my feet crossed, am I necessarily suggesting that the person I am showing must sit in the chair in the same position, or is the intended example focused on the computer task? As in all communication, we need common sense as we infer significance and discern between the purpose of the example and the incidental details in the telling of the event.

In Acts 20, when the disciples came together on the first day of the week to break bread (the Lord's Supper), was the focus of this on their meeting in an upper room, or is the intended focus on their meeting to break bread? Where they met is incidental. What they met for is integral, and we need to see that difference. We need common sense, keeping passages in context and recognizing the difference between an incidental of telling what happened and core issues that led to the disciples acting as they did in the first place. Are we capable of drawing reasonable conclusions about these? We do that in our normal communication. Are we not capable here?

God chose to include examples of His people acting for a reason. Those who love Him ought to look at those examples and, as much as within their abilities, and where the circumstances compare, follow them. Why ask, "Do I have to?" (i.e., "Is it binding?") When God has, in His wisdom, provided a look into the actions that He likes, those who love Him should want to do the same. That's a foundational starting point from which the particular examples can be examined. From there we can consider how comparable the examples are to our circumstances. If our circumstances are not very comparable (e.g., specific issues with miraculous gifts), then we may have little application to make of that specific case. No example can be followed when there is no comparable situation to which we can apply it. If it is comparable, then in what ways? What is the context of the example and how does it fit with our context? Is it an example of individual or group action? What is the core issue of the example? What are the incidentals? What shall we take away from it? How may we apply it? These are the types of questions we want to consider.

Acts 20:7 as an Example

The disciples gathered together on the first day of the week in order to "break bread." This shows both timing and purpose, and context implies more than just a common meal intended. Acts 2:42 shows that disciples "were continually devoting themselves to the apostles' teaching and to fellowship, to the breaking of bread and to prayer." This was not just an ordinary meal or secular gathering.

Elsewhere Paul refers to the Lord's Supper in this way: "Is not the cup of blessing which we bless a sharing in the blood of Christ? Is not the bread which we break a sharing in the body of Christ? Since there is one bread, we who are many are one body; for we all partake of the one bread" (1 Cor. 10:16-17). Partaking of the "one bread" and "the bread which we break" refer to the sharing in the body of Christ in this special meal. We know that God desires for Christians to partake of the Lord's Supper, since the Lord commanded it (Matt. 26:26-29; 1 Cor. 11:23-26). Both biblically and historically, we know that disciples met on the first day of the week for this purpose. Paul and his company stayed seven days at Troas in order to do this (cf. also Acts 21:4; 28:14). That the first day of the week was the common meeting day is seen also in passages like 1 Corinthians 16:1-2, where the instructions presuppose that they met on this day regularly. The first day of the week makes sense since it was both the day that Christ rose from the dead and the day of Pentecost on which the Holy Spirit came with power in order to usher in the new era of the church. Acts 2:42 implies that they began breaking bread in this way on that Pentecost, and continued regularly doing so. "For as often as you eat this bread and drink the cup, you proclaim the Lord's death until He comes" (1 Cor. 11:26).

We see "first day of the week" significance in both what we are told and shown. We know nothing of other days that disciples met to partake of the Lord's Supper because we have no other information given to us about it. Jesus gave instructions on the Passover, but He said He would later partake of it in His kingdom, which takes us again to the day of Pentecost. The only example we have when disciples came together to take the Lord's Supper is on the first day of the week. This is what God shows us, and this is what the Christians, with God's approval, did in the first century. Can we agree on this and practice it? Should we do more than that?

Conclusion

Examples are an important part of Scripture. Through them, God shows us what He likes or doesn't like. If we are able, and if our circumstances are comparable, then we ought to follow these examples. Further, we ought to act based upon what we know from what we are told and shown, not on what we don't know due to what God hasn't revealed. Loving God, will we choose to act on what we see God showing us and teach others the same?

Discussion Questions

1. Why is a pattern significant when we want to know how to do something? *It gives a model to follow*

2. How do examples illustrate what God likes or doesn't like? *Examples show what is acceptable to Him. He chosen*

3. Why is asking, "Is that example binding?" probably not the best question to ask as a starting point? What kind of attitude might that reveal? *Do we have to? ~~Week~~ Week unengaged. Forced, Lazy, not committed.*

4. How can we know that God is pleased when we follow particular examples in Scripture? *Because God gave them to us. They were carried out by His apostles.*

5. What should our starting attitude be as we consider any given example, and why? *Let see what God desires? We should look for ways that God has shown us how to live for Him*

6. Why is it important to consider whether the context of an example is comparable to our circumstances today? *If it applies to the situation. If it doesn't don't force to.*

7. Why is an example, like the one found in Acts 20:7, important to us now? *It gives us the time and way to partake of the Lords Supper. Who to share it with*

8. What indicators do we have that the first day of the week is a day God wants disciples meeting? *Because the day the apostles met was always the first day of the week. They stayed 7 days in Thos so they could meet and do this. Also the day of resurrection and pentecost.*

Silence

God reigns. Because of this, His followers need to be concerned with teaching God's will. "Whoever speaks, is to do so as one who is speaking the utterances of God" (1 Pet. 4:11a). Yet how are we to think with respect to what God didn't say?

The question of how to treat the silence of Scripture has long been one of the more controversial issues in determining what is or is not authorized by God. Does silence authorize? Do we have authority to act when God has said nothing? There are two basic approaches to silence: 1) we can do anything not specifically forbidden in Scripture, or 2) silence is not permission and we should not do something that is not positively indicated in some way. How shall we approach the issue?

Interpreting "Silence" or the "Unspecified"?

We need to distinguish between something that is generally authorized, even though unspecified, and something for which there is actual silence. "Silent" and "unspecified" are not equal. For example, I can send my son to the store with the instructions to "get bread." "Bread" is a category, so if nothing else is indicated to specify the kind of bread, then whatever fits the category of "bread" is permitted. That is different, however, from saying or indicating nothing (silence) about bread whatsoever. If something is stated in principle or in general terms, then whatever falls under that principle or generality is still within the context of what is spoken about. Not everything needs to be specified when a general principle is given that covers the specifics.

That said, silence is silence. It is nothing. It neither approves nor disapproves of anything in itself. However, we cannot quote an author on something he never said. This is a basic principle on which we normally operate. If we cite an author as approving something, we must be able to show where and how he spoke about it. Otherwise, we have misrepresented the author. When an author has said nothing about a subject, we have no warrant to say that he approves of the matter. An author "authorizes" by what he says, not by his silence, unless he has indicated otherwise. For example, singing is authorized in Ephesians 5:19. Those who want approval for mechanical instruments in worship will need to go elsewhere, for this passage says nothing about instruments.

If the author has not said anything about a subject, does that necessarily mean he disapproves? The only way to know this would be for the author to break his silence and indicate His will. How else could we know? Once he breaks his silence, this point is no longer at issue. However, imagine the author saying something like this: "I'm only approving of or promoting matters that I have spoken about. I do not approve of anything else. Do not presume so." Then, when he is silent about something, what should we assume his feelings to be about it? We surely cannot assume that he approves of something he has not spoken about; in that case, based on what else he has told us, we need to assume he would not approve it. This leads to the next point:

Silence and the Problem of Presumption

Interpreting "silence" is easier when we see someone. We can see facial and bodily expressions, hear inflections in the way things are said, and be more aware of what a communicator might be trying to convey. A speaker can say something with a particular expression and we can more readily interpret what that means. In biblical interpretation, our challenge lies in the fact that we are reading a text without being able to see all the accompanying expressions that may or may not go with it. This lends itself to the problem of presumption and warrants a more careful approach.

Presumption is assuming something to be true when we may not have adequate grounds for accepting it. Indeed, the evidence may be in the other direction, but because we think, "Scripture is silent on that specific matter," we believe we can act. Or we may think, "that's a gray area, so I can go ahead and do it." Instead of being sure what we are doing is right, we presume that it's okay. This is dangerous ground to be avoided.

Even if real silence didn't prohibit (as many argue), it surely doesn't authorize. Why do we feel that we can presume upon silence to act? The mind of God is known through what is revealed (1 Cor. 2:10-13). If God truly is silent about a matter, there would only be a couple of reasons why this would be so: 1) He intends to be silent. In this case, we do not have the mind of God on the matter, and we can either presume upon His mind, or refrain from such presumption. Given the principles of honoring God in Scripture, which is more appropriate? We know the answer. 2) He intended to say something about the issue, but failed or forgot. This is not an option because it would make God incompetent. If God truly is silent, then He intended to be silent and we ought to respect that.

When considering the question of silence, we ought to bear in mind these principles: First, study all that God has revealed about an issue. Consider relevant principles, statements, or examples that cover what we are trying to address. Only by knowing what God has revealed are we able to determine whether or not He is silent about something. Second, always keep in mind the need to honor God in what we think and do. Failure to honor Him has gotten more than a few people into serious trouble (e.g., Nabad and Abihu in Lev. 10:1-3, and Moses in Num. 20:9-13).

Fallacy, Principle, and Silence.

What is wise? What will please God?

In logic, there is a fallacy known as the *appeal to ignorance* (*Ad Ignorantiam*): "The 'appeal to ignorance' consists in arguing that an idea must be true because we do not know that it is not. It is a fallacy because ignorance can never be a premise or reason. Premises must express knowledge-claims. Nothing logically follows from nothing, I.e., no-knowledge" (Kreeft 86). Using silence as a basis for God's authority is fallacious and presumptuous.

There are several principles that prohibit this type of fallacy and help us understand how God thinks about this.

Need to look carefully at what is revealed.

- "Whatever I command you, you shall be careful to do; you shall not add to nor take away from it" (Deut. 12:32).
- "The secret things belong to the Lord our God, but the things revealed belong to us and to our sons forever, that we may observe all the words of this law" (Deut. 29:29).
- "Do not add to His words or He will reprove you, and you will be proved a liar" (Prov. 30:6).
- "Be strong and courageous, for you shall give this people possession of the land which I swore to their fathers to give them. Only be strong and very courageous; be careful to do according to all the law which Moses My servant commanded you; do not turn from it to the right or to the left, so that you may have success wherever you go" (Josh. 1:6-7; cf. Deut. 5:32; 17:11).
- "When they say to you, 'Consult the mediums and the spiritists who whisper and mutter,' should not a people consult their God? Should they consult the dead on behalf of the living? To the law and to the testimony! If they do not speak according to this word, it is because they have no dawn." (Isa. 8:19-20).
- "But one who looks intently at the perfect law, the law of liberty, and abides by it, not having become a forgetful hearer but an effectual doer, this man will be blessed in what he does" (Jas. 1:25).
- "So Jesus was saying to those Jews who had believed Him, 'If you continue in My word, then you are truly disciples of

Mine; and you will know the truth, and the truth will make you free'" (John 8:31-32).

- "Now these things, brethren, I have figuratively applied to myself and Apollos for your sakes, so that in us you may learn not to exceed what is written, so that no one of you will become arrogant in behalf of one against the other" (1 Cor. 4:6).

- "Anyone who goes too far and does not abide in the teaching of Christ, does not have God; the one who abides in the teaching, he has both the Father and the Son" (2 John 9).

- "I testify to everyone who hears the words of the prophecy of this book: if anyone adds to them, God will add to him the plagues which are written in this book; and if anyone takes away from the words of the book of this prophecy, God will take away his part from the tree of life and from the holy city, which are written in this book" (Rev. 22:18-19).

- "Since we have heard that some of our number to whom we gave no instruction have disturbed you with their words, unsettling your souls…" (Acts 15:24).

- "If anyone advocates a different doctrine and does not agree with sound words, those of our Lord Jesus Christ, and with the doctrine conforming to godliness, he is conceited and understands nothing …" (1 Tim. 6:3-4ff, vv. 20-21).

Examine the contexts. Some of the references have specific points to be made about them, but we are showing a basic principle throughout Scriptures found in various contexts (law, history, wisdom, prophets, gospels, and epistles). Do we recognize the principle? Do we get the idea that God thinks this principle is important? What might we gather from what we know? Are we being too careful, or not careful enough about our speculations and filling in of the gaps?

Conclusion

While the question of God's silence can be thorny, we need to start with how we understand silence in our normal communication. From there, we look at other principles that help us in our understanding of silence. In the case of God, we have very direct statements telling us what He thinks about our being presumptuous. Therefore, we must be very careful in our approach to any question on which God is silent.

Discussion Questions

1. Why is the distinction between "silence" and "unspecified" important? *generally authorized "unspecified" Silence nothing is said about the matter*

2. If an author says nothing about a topic, what should we assume about his position on the topic, and why? *He has not given info into that topic he neither agrees or disagrees*

3. Why is presumption a problem? *it's nothing You're probably trying to justify your own actions.*

4. How do we know what God thinks about a particular matter? *Study what He has revealed*

5. If God is truly silent about a matter, what reasons might there be for this silence? *He intended to be silent*

6. What is the "appeal to ignorance" fallacy and why is it significant for the issue of silence? *an idea must be true because we do not know it is not.*

7. Given the passages listed, what should we conclude regarding God's attitude toward what He has not revealed? *It is lies and arrogance.*

8. How careful should we be in approaching questions involving silence, and why? *Very careful. God has given very direct statement regarding being presumptuous.*

The Church of the Lord

As Creator and King, Jesus is also Head of His body, the church (Col. 1:15-18). As His body, we are to listen to the Head and respond accordingly. We have considered basic principles in understanding the way that God communicates His will. He communicates in the same way that we communicate with others: at the most basic level, He tells us what He wants, shows us what He wants, and implies what He expects us to get. Now we want to think about what God has revealed about His church. What is the church? Why is the local church important? What activities do we find in Scripture that God wants the local church to be involved in?

What the Church is Not

It's often helpful not only to positively state what the church is, but also, for clarity, to state what it is not. Since there is much misinformation regarding the church, let's start with what the church is not:

First the church is not the building. We know this, but we need to be careful with the way we express ourselves.

Second, the church is not a denomination. Many have the idea that belonging to a church necessarily means belonging to some denomination. This is false. Denominationalism finds no support in Scripture, and our plea is not to leave one denomination to join another, but to abandon all denominationalism and simply be part of Christ's body.

Third, the church is not a social club. While there are many social benefits to being able to spend time with other Christians in spiritual and even social settings, the church was not designed as a social organization meant to provide for all social and physical needs, take care of entertainment, and make sure everyone is socially happy. Not even Jesus was concerned about fixing every social situation. For example, Luke 12:13-15 presents a situation where two brothers had a dispute over a family inheritance. Jesus could have easily solved the situation, but notice his reply: "Man, who appointed Me a judge or arbitrator over you?" His purpose was not to fix all the social, political, or financial problems in society. Further, in John 6:26-27, Jesus had already fed the people, but He was not willing for that to be the premise upon which they would follow Him. They needed to move beyond the signs and the food to accept the teachings of Jesus. Many ended up walking away because of what Jesus said in John 6.

Fourth, the church is not a political conduit. Jesus brought together disciples who were on very different ends of a political spectrum: Simon, a zealot and Matthew, a tax collector. The local church does not exist in order to be a political machine aimed at promoting various political agendas. There should be no attempt in a local congregational setting to overthrow a government or become lobbyists for particular political campaigns. Scripture teaches Christians to submit to governing authorities (Rom. 13) and not to speak evil of those in charge, but to pray for them so that we lead a peaceful life (cf. Jude 8-9; 1 Tim. 2:1-4).

Following the example of Jesus and the early church, we see that the primary function of a local church is spiritual in nature, focused on helping people draw near to God. The drawing power of what we offer is the cross of Jesus (John 12:32). We need to make sure we don't undermine this by making physical agendas the primary function. None of this means that Christians should avoid their personal responsibilities to help those in need, take care of the sick, or feed the hungry (cf. Jas. 1:26-27; Gal. 6:10). It does mean that we need to keep a proper perspective about priorities.

The Meaning of "Church" (*Ekklesia*)

Put simply, *the church is a group of people*. In the context of God's people, it refers to those who are saved by the blood of Christ (cf. Acts 20:28). Many argue that the term *ekklesia*, usually translated "church," was etymologically derived from *ek*, "out of," and *klesis*, "a calling," thus referring to those who are "called out." However, "called out" is not the primary significance of the term in Scripture. We should not confuse etymology (origin of a word) with usage. The main idea of *ekklesia* is that of an "assembly," "group," or "Congregation." For example, the term is used of the assembly of citizens who were gathered to discuss certain affairs of a potentially riotous mob (Acts 19:32, 39, 41). It is also used of Israel in the wilderness (Acts 7:38), showing that it is not limited to Christians in the New Testament. The term is not inherently religious.

Specifically, we find the term *ekklesia* used, when referring to Christians, with at least the following senses:

Universally, *ekklesia* refers to all of God's people without specifying a time or place (Matt. 16:18; Heb. 12:23). There is no specific locality for the assembly and no organization of the universal group. It is broad and general in scope. Whether living in the first century or twenty-first century, or whether living in Europe, Africa, or America, all of God's people are part of this general assembly. It is dependent upon one's individual relationship to God. God has given no organization or collective activity to this group. Action can only be taken individually as there is no universal function other than Christians being what they are supposed to be.

Locally, *ekklesia* refers to a specified group of believers who have banded together to carry out God's work in a particular community or city (e.g., 1 Cor. 1:2). A local church is an organized, independent group of God's people with leaders (e.g., Phil. 1:1). It has no organizational ties to other independent groups, and it does not answer to other groups. In a plurality, "churches" refers to more than one local group rather than different denominations (Rom. 16:16; Gal. 1:2; cf. Rev. 1:4, 20 with 2:1, 8, 12, 18; 3:1, 7, 14). Even when we aren't meeting at a particular moment, we are members of the group that meet in that location. We don't cease to be the local church when we depart from a physical assembly.

Locally, *when the church is physically assembled* together for specific action (e.g., to worship), then *ekklesia* applies to that gathered assembly (e.g., 1 Cor. 11:18; 14:19, 23). The church comes together in assemblies with the express purposes of carrying out God's will for the local group.

Jesus is the Head of the church, both universally and locally (Col. 1:18; Eph. 1:22-23). Individuals, not sub-groups, comprise the universal body as well as the local body (Rom. 12:4-5). Universally, there is only one body that belongs to Christ (Eph. 4:4), whereas locally there are many groups in multiple locations. While there is no universal organization, as if all churches are under some earthly headquarters, there is local organization wherein a congregation acts independently to the glory of God with its own leadership (Heb. 13:17).

When did this church universally begin? The Lord promised He would build His church (Matt. 16:18). This is not to imply that God did not have a group of believers before Jesus (cf. Heb. 11-12), but that the new covenant would be in effect soon and the new company of believers would be established in a new relationship under this new and better covenant (See Heb. 8:7-13). Christ uses the figure of a building structure to refer to His people under the new covenant. This should highlight the idea that God's people are His temple (cf. 1 Pet. 2:5, 9; Eph. 2:19-22; 1 Cor. 3:9-17). After Christ died and rose again, and on the Day of Pentecost, the Lord was adding people to His body of believers (Acts 2:47). Locally, churches begin in different places and at different times.

Several figures are used to refer to God's people in the New Testament, such as "body" (Eph. 1:22-23; Col. 1:18), "household" (1 Tim. 3:15), and "temple" (1 Cor. 3:16). The church's relationship to the Lord is compared to a bride and her husband (Eph. 5:22-33; Rev. 21:2). These, and more, point to the type of relationship we have with God and each other in Christ. Yet God did not specify a single title for this body of believers. Descriptions are given which identify the church as belonging to God (Acts 20:28) and Christ (Rom. 16:16, where "churches of Christ" refers to several local groups); other descriptions refer to a specific locality ("church of God which is at Corinth," 1 Cor. 1:2; Rev. 2-3), or as being composed of Christians in a given location ("church of the Thessalonians," 1 Thess. 1:1). Hebrews 12:23 refers to the "church of the first-born ones" (plural), which shows the exalted position to which God elevates believers. All such phrases are descriptive. We need to be careful that we don't just single out one exclusive title, as this itself would be going beyond the authority presented in Scripture.

Conclusion

The church universally and churches locally all exist by the authority of God. There are many misconceptions about the church, so it is important to understand both what the church is and what it is not. Once we understand the various uses of "church" in Scripture, we will then be in a position to understand better why the church exists.

Discussion Questions

1. Why should we be careful about not confusing the church with the building in which the church meets?

2. Why should we learn not to think of the church as a denomination, a social club, or a political conduit?

3. What is meant by "universal church"? Where do we find this concept in Scripture? Is this a physically organized group?

4. What is the main idea of *ekklesia*, and why is this important to understand?

5. Why is it important to recognize that a local church operates independently of other local churches or organizations?

6. Who comprises the universal body with Christ as the Head, and why is this an important understanding?

7. What is the difference between the universal church and local churches in terms of when they began?

8. Why should we be careful not to use only one designation for the church exclusively?

Why the Church Exists

Jesus Christ is head of the body, the church (Col. 1:18). This means that we need to be concerned with His will for what the church is supposed to be and why it exists. We have seen that "church" (*ekklesia*) refers to a group of people, whether universally, locally, or physically assembled. Now the question is, why does the church exist? Our primary concern here is to consider the reason for a local congregation. Why do local churches need to exist, and what is God's work for them? What has God authorized with respect to a local congregation?

Evidence for the Local Group

Some have denied the importance of an organized local church, so let's first consider the evidence for localized congregational activity. First is the fact that specific epistles are addressed to local congregations (1 Cor. 1:2; Gal. 1:1; 2 Cor. 1:1; 8:1; Phil. 1:1; Col. 1:2; 1 Thess. 1:1; 2 Thess. 1:1; Rev. 2-3). These epistles would be read to the church when they assembled. Within the context of the local group, funds were collected (cf. Acts 5:1-6; 1 Cor. 16:1-3), and regular meetings occurred where they worshiped together and partook of the Lord's Supper together (1 Cor. 11:17-34; 14; Acts 20:7). The local group is charged with particular action, or, in some cases, to refrain from particular action. For example, when it comes to the care of "widows indeed," the church was not to be burdened (1 Tim. 5:16); rather, individuals needed to take care of their own (1 Tim. 5:3-4).

These passages, and more, can only make sense in the context of a local congregational organization. Contrasted with the universal body, which has no set organization, a local group will often have, with the saints in that place, "overseers and deacons" (Phil. 1:1).

These overseers, or elders, are responsible to shepherd the group over which they have the charge (Acts 20:28; 1 Pet. 5:2-3; Heb. 13:17). They are not universal shepherds, but only local.

These passages further show that God wants Christians involved in a local congregation. We need to avoid the extreme of thinking that the local church is unimportant and that only the individual matters. While the church is comprised of individuals, and individuals function within the group (Eph. 4:16), the group as a whole unit is also a gift from God for the effective working of His will. At the same time, we need to be careful about confining Christianity to the "institution" so that the individual fails to work as God directs.

God wants local groups to exist, but why? What is it about local assemblies of Christians that make them so valuable and desirable? First, a group that can band together to help each other in their service to God is going to make one stronger than if the individual tries to do it all alone. This purpose is expressed in the well-known passage: "Let us hold fast the confession of our hope without wavering, for He who promised is faithful; and let us consider how to stimulate one another to love and good deeds, not forsaking our own assembling together, as is the habit of some, but encouraging one another; and all the more as you see the day drawing near" (Heb. 10:23-25). The stress here is not just assembling, but assembling for the purpose of encouraging each other so that when we leave the assembly we'll be motivated to love and do good works. Encouragement is one significant reason why we need each other in a local body.

Scripture also shows that when local Christians band together in order to function as a local group, whether through the pooling of funds or assembling together (1 Cor. 11:18; 14:23), God has particular actions in mind for His people. Coming together "as a church" is an important concept.

In these cases, "church" refers to a specific body of believers who have banded together and agreed to work and function together in activities that God intended for that setting. As an analogy, think of a family, which is fitting given that God's people are God's household. A family can be dispersed, but still be a family. That family can also assemble and act as a family unit for specific ends. So it is with the church. The church is composed of individuals, but locally a church exists as a unit for particular purposes.

Groups or organizations often form for specific reasons. For example, a hospital may be built and staffed with doctors, nurses, and administration, and we recognize that the hospital organization does not exist as such in order to have political rallies or provide the world with donuts. Those who give to the hospital would likely be upset if they found that the money being donated was used for purposes other than what was intended. If individuals thought they were giving to an organization that was intended to feed hungry children and later found out the money was being spent to buy softball equipment, they would rightly have a problem with this misuse of funds. Why should this be any different when it comes to a local church?

The local church, as an organized group, exists for specific reasons, which is not to be confused with all other sorts of purposes and activities that can be handled in other venues and situations. For instance, the local church does not exist to provide secular education and hand out degrees. These things aren't wrong in themselves, but it would be outside the scope of congregational purpose to provide these. The local church has a more specific and important work to do that other organizations do not do. When we say that the local church should stay out of certain activities, we are not saying that Christians as individuals and families cannot provide for those activities. On the contrary, there is a difference between individual and congregational action. Recognizing that distinction is important. This is highlighted in 1 Timothy 5, where individuals are told to care for their own widows so that the church is not burdened (vs. 16).

The Actions of a Local Group

What are the specified actions that we find given to the local group who function "as a church" in Scripture? One primary function is that the local group participates in and supports the preaching of the gospel. For example, the church of the Thessalonians was commended because "the word of the Lord has sounded forth" from them (1 Thess. 1:7-8). The church at Philippi is commended because they, as a church, had fellowship with Paul in supporting him as he preached (Phil. 4:15-16). Since preachers have a right to make their living of the gospel (1 Cor. 9:14), and churches can help in the support of preachers, we find in this one of the main reasons for a local church to exist.

The local group functions further in the spiritual edification or building up of the saved. This is teaching that is intended to strengthen the faith and resolve of believers. Paul shows that saints are to be taught to serve. The fact that evangelists, pastors, and teachers are mentioned in this setting shows that there is a local church context for this (Eph. 4:11-16). When Paul addressed the Ephesian elders, he told them to watch over that local flock because savage wolves (false teachers) would come in and not spare them. Therefore, the word of God's grace needed to be taught diligently among them (Acts 20:17-32). This is a reason why churches typically have Bible classes, wherein they can teach what is needed to those in differing stages of growth and understanding.

The local group works in helping to provide for saints who are in physical need. While it would be nice to be able to provide benevolence to the whole world, or even to a whole city, that kind of work is neither possible nor found within the pages of Scripture. In Scripture, where the local church organization is involved, benevolence was intended for needy saints (Acts 2:44-46; 4:33-35; 6:1-6; 11:27-30; 1 Cor. 16:1-2; 2 Cor. 8:1-4; 2 Cor. 9; Rom. 15:25-26; 1 Tim. 5:9-16). Yet even this was largely temporary. The group is responsible for taking care of its own first, then may also, if able, help saints elsewhere in need. Remember, we are speaking here of local church action, not what individual Christians may do from their own personal circumstances and opportunities. Group activity is necessarily more limited than individual activity because of purpose and work (cf. Acts 5:4). This, again, is true of all purposeful organizations.

The local group also maintains local assemblies wherein the saints seek to worship and praise God together. While this is also part of the edification process, the point here is that God's people ought to gather together regularly in order to worship Him and care for the specified actions shown in God's will (cf. Acts 2:42). In this context will be found coming together as a church in order to participate together in the Lord's Supper (1 Cor. 11:18ff; Acts 20:7), thereby sharing in the body and blood of the Lord (1 Cor. 10:16).

Conclusion

Understanding these basic principles concerning the church will help us in our further study of authority, especially as it relates to the work and mission God has given the church. Local churches need to focus on the spiritual nature of God's kingdom, and the spiritual mission of His people. Acting as a collective unit is important, as Scripture demonstrates. At the same time, Christians should discern between work that God has given the local body and what He expects from the individual and family.

Discussion Questions

1. What evidence do we have in Scripture that organized, local churches existed in the first century?

2. Why is the evidence for the local churches important? What does it show us?

3. Why is a local congregation so valuable to the spiritual well-being of the Christian?

4. Why is it important to recognize the local church, as such, exists as a purposeful organization for specific work?

5. How does a local group participate in the preaching of the gospel (e.g., Phil. 4:15-16)?

6. What is the purpose of edification and why is it so important to the work of a congregation?

7. What biblical grounds are there for a church to provide benevolent help to needy saints?

8. Overall, what have you learned about the importance of a local church and the Christian's relationship to one?

How the Church Works

Recognizing the kingship and headship of Christ (Col. 1:18) also means recognizing the importance of His will in how a local church is going to work. Previously, we saw four areas in Scripture in which the local group is to function: fellowship in preaching to the lost, edifying and strengthening the saved, helping to provide benevolent help to saints in physical need, and maintaining collective worship to God. We have also seen that the work is primarily spiritual in nature. While there are social benefits to being a part of a local congregation, the reason for its existence is to do the spiritual work of God. As God's people in a given locality, every congregation has a spiritual work to perform. This work should not be compromised by shifting the focus to recreational, social, or political issues. This lesson will consider scriptural ways in which the work of the local group is to be accomplished.

Principles About Collective Funds

Since funds are necessarily involved in carrying out the work of the local church (nothing is free), principles about those funds are also important. The local church work is going to be funded by the free will offerings of the members of that congregation (cf. 1 Cor. 16:1-2; 2 Cor. 9:6-8). This is not a forced tithe, and the New Testament nowhere gives a percentage for giving. Rather, Christians give as they prosper, willingly and cheerfully, knowing they are having fellowship in matters pertaining to God and His kingdom.

Is there biblical authority for a collective treasury to exist? Let's consider the evidence. In Acts 4:36-37 and 5:1-2, money was laid at apostles' feet, which implies that the apostles gained control of the collective funds in Jerusalem once they were given by the Christians. That is, essentially, a treasury. Paul, in 1 Corinthians

16:1-3, gives directions to the local group and shows other local groups received the same instructions (vs. 1). Christians were to "put aside and save, that no collections be made when I come." If they did not pool their funds, then collections would have to be taken up when Paul arrived, which is not what he wanted. Paul spoke of the collection as "your gift" (singular) in verse 3. It was a collective gift, again implying a group collection all in one place. Then, in Philippians 4:15-16, we find that the group at Philippi supported Paul in his preaching. The support is said to be from that local group, not just select individuals. The only way this would make much sense is if they had pooled their funds together in some way (cf. also 2 Cor. 11:8).

Once funds are pooled together, they become the property of the group and are purposed for specified work. In Acts 5:1-4, Ananias retained control of his property and funds until he surrendered it to the group. His sin here was lying about what or how much he gave. Whatever we contribute for group use falls under the control of the group, not just one individual. The funds so collected do not belong to the individual any more, but are dedicated for the group's work.

Any legitimate organization knows that when 1) the organization exists for a particular purpose, and 2) funds are given by its members in order to facilitate that purpose, then it stands to reason that the purpose for which an organization exists and for which it collects funds is also what limits how those funds ought to be spent. Misuse of funds (using them for purposes other than stated intent) is a serious charge (even a crime) in the business world as it goes right to the integrity of those who run the business. This is well understood in secular circles. All we are doing now is applying the same, logical principle to the purpose for which a local church organization exists and for which funds are collected and dispersed.

The application of the principle is as follows: since the group is authorized by God to work in certain ways, then the distribution of the group funds are limited by the purpose for which the group exists (which comes from Scripture). A congregation does not have biblical authority to spend the money any way the leaders desire. The funds are limited by the work which God has authorized it to do; however the funds are spent indicates how the Christians work as a collective unit.

Since a local church is authorized to share in the preaching of the gospel, the collected funds may be spent in whatever is necessary and expedient to do the work — support preachers, provide materials, etc. Since God has not specified every aspect of this, there is some choice as to whom a group may support (assuming the man is teaching truth) and what materials it may procure to facilitate that work. However, if the leaders take those funds and arbitrarily spend them on movie tickets, ball games, or something else unrelated to the work, people would rightly challenge the unauthorized action and subsequently seek proper authority. The same would be true for edification, benevolence, and worship.

The Direct Nature of the Work

There is no indication in Scripture that a local church, by donating their collective funds, went through a para-church organization or institution that did the work on their behalf. No Scripture indicates that a local congregation should be an agency for collecting donations that then go to other organizations. There are no middle-man agencies, collecting funds and making the decisions, between the church and the work being done. Bear in mind that there is no universal organization given in the Scriptures. The universal church, which includes all Christians from all times and all locations, cannot be universally activated or organized.

Local groups are not structurally tied to another organization, nor are they tied to each other through organized centralization. Local groups are independent and autonomous (self-governing, not ruled by other churches or organizations). Congregations were similar as a result of teaching the same doctrine (e.g., 1 Cor. 14:33; 16:1), but they were not organizationally tied to each other. Centralization attempts to activate universal organization and is a component of denominationalism, which is an organized body of religious congregations (i.e., the congregations comprise the body rather than the individuals). This is nowhere found in Scripture.

Each local group in the New Testament collected and disbursed its own funds. While one church may send to another in the case of saints in physical need, there is nothing that shows one church collecting funds from other churches because they decided to do some work that they couldn't afford. There is no scriptural indication that one eldership or institution should seek to take and oversee funds of another congregation. Elders can only, legitimately, shepherd the flock "among you" (that is, over their own local group, 1 Pet. 5:2-3). Following, we will see this principle applied in the specified works of local congregations:

In the preaching of the gospel. A local group can and should support gospel preachers. The Scriptures show that such support was sent or given directly to the preacher (Phil. 4:15-16; 2 Cor. 11:8). Support was not funneled through another congregation ("sponsoring church"), missionary society, or college that, in turn, decided who to support and how to use the funds.

In the work of edification. The principle is the same for edification and worship. The local group provides the place, people, and provisions for doing the work. In this way, the group "edifies itself" and is not dependent upon other institutions or organizations to do what they ought to be doing for themselves. Each member is to be taught to serve (Eph. 5:11) so that the group is "fitted and held together by what every joint supplies, according to the proper working of each individual part" that "causes the growth of the body for the building up of itself in love" (Eph. 4:16).

In the work of benevolence. A local group has first obligation to its own members (cf. 1 Cor. 12:12-26), and so provides help when there is a saint in physical need. Acts 6 shows how the church at Jerusalem handled this kind of situation within their own group. It was not done by collecting funds to funnel or donate into another institution, which in turn provided for itself and other needs according to its own discretion and oversight. Rather, the local group maintained its own work and oversight. When a local group cannot adequately provide its own needs (such as in a wide-spread famine), the Scriptures show that one group may send relief to another group (Acts 11:27-30; Rom. 15:25-27). Again, this is direct relief, not funneled through another institution that makes the decisions. This is a temporary situation intended to help stabilize the needy saints in that location (2 Cor. 8:1, 14). This is the only scriptural circumstance we find in which one group sends funds to another. The funds are not redistributed to another institution once it reaches its destination. The group in need then handles what they receive from others.

Conclusion

The way in which we see local churches operating in Scripture is not difficult. There are no complicated hierarchies. There are no centralized organizations making decisions for all the churches. Each local group handles its own work, its own needs, and its own resources. When a church used funds, they sent directly to the work, whether it be a preacher or a needy group when the situation called for it. There were no middle organizations collecting donations to take care of the work for the churches. The independent nature of each congregation reflects the wisdom of God and local groups are wise in maintaining their local work in the same way that is shown in Scripture.

Discussion Questions

1. Why is it important for a congregation to pay careful attention to the way its funds are spent?

2. When an individual gives to the church, what happens in principle with those funds? Why is this important?

3. What do secular organizations understand about spending funds given to them? How does this analogy help us in thinking about congregational spending?

4. Why is the centralization of several churches a problem scripturally?

5. When a local group supported a preacher (like Paul), how did they do it?

6. Read Ephesians 4:11-16 again. How should a congregation seek to do the work of edification?

7. When benevolence is needed, how was the work accomplished both 1) locally, and 2) with respect to helping other groups?

8. Does it matter how a local church proceeds with its work? Why or why not?

Worship and Assembly

"Ascribe to the Lord the glory due to His name; worship the Lord in holy array" (Psalm 29:2).

God has always been in charge of what pleases Him in worship. Is any and all worship acceptable to God? If all worship is acceptable, what is the biblical basis for thinking so? If all worship is not acceptable, then on what basis should we proceed in worship? God was not just against worshiping other gods (Deut. 5:9). He was also concerned with how worship was conducted (e.g., Neh. 12:45); reverence was always expected (cf. Psalm 2:11). If we are going to be God's people, then we need to pay attention to these concerns.

Should our concern not be to offer up spiritual sacrifices that God accepts? Peter wrote, "you also, as living stones, are being built up as a spiritual house for a holy priesthood, to offer up spiritual sacrifices acceptable to God through Jesus Christ" (1 Peter 2:5). There are spiritual sacrifices through Jesus that God accepts. Does it imply that there might be some forms of worship and sacrifice that are not acceptable?

Basic Meaning of Worship

Some seem to view worship as confined to a place and time: "Where do you worship?" "What time is worship?" Worship is much more. It is action coupled with attitude. However, worship is not dependent on a place now, but upon the proper application of "truth and spirit" (John 4:21-24). God has always wanted worship from the heart, so if our hearts are not right, then no worship has occurred regardless of the motions we go through (Matt. 15:8). We might say the right words yet our hearts be far from God, rendering our worship vain.

Terms in Scripture indicating worship involve revering, honoring, and fearing God. The word *Proskuneo* means to prostrate oneself before something (or someone) as an act of reverence, fear, or supplication (Louw and Nida 218). This is used in John 4:24. To worship God means that we revere and honor Him, bowing ourselves before Him in service and attitude. This implies that we must worship God as He directs, for we cannot honor Him without listening to His will (Matt. 7:21-23). We must not subjectively do whatever we want then call it "worship." Revering and honoring God means that we do what He says (Luke 6:46; Eccl. 12:13).

God is in charge of worship. There were specified "regulations of divine worship and the earthly sanctuary" (Heb. 9:1), and the people were not to deviate from them. He was clear that they were not to worship other gods (Deut. 4:19; 5:9; 6:13; 8:19). He had the tabernacle built according to a strict pattern (Exod. 25:40 ; 1 Chron. 28:11ff). This included the priesthood, sacrifices, instruments, and anything else connected to the tabernacle (or temple) worship (see Neh. 12:45). When individuals bowed in reverence and honored God, this was also called worship (Judges 7:15). The worshiper reveres and honors God, does what God says, and avoids worshiping anything else.

Collective Activities in Assembly and Worship

There are activities that God desires for us to do collectively when assembled (this is not saying that every action must be done in every single assembly; for example, we might assemble for prayer or song). These activities are forms of service and honor to Him because we find them revealed in His will. When we do them as He has directed, and with a proper heart, then we are worshiping. (Please note that this is not dealing with an individual worshiping at home, though the individual still needs to be careful to honor and revere God appropriately outside the assembly).

There are some areas of collective activities as worship to God. Some refer to "five acts of worship," but we need to be careful that we are not turning the idea into some kind of cold ritual or checklist. Everything we do in our collective actions that are meant to glorify and honor God would fall under the umbrella of worship or offering up acceptable sacrifices through Jesus Christ. Here, then, in no particular order, are activities that we find the Christians doing when gathered together "as a church":

They partook of the the Lord's Supper on the first day of the week (Acts 20:7). The Lord put this in the assembly as a joint participation with other saints (1 Cor. 11:18ff). When we take the Lord's Supper, we are honoring and revering God for what He has done on our behalf. In this action, we are: remembering and proclaiming the death of Christ (1 Cor. 11:24, 26); looking forward to His return (1 Cor. 11:26); examining ourselves (1 Cor. 11:28); judging the body of Christ (1 Cor. 11:29); and communing with Jesus and each other (1 Cor. 10:16).

They prayed together. We are to pray individually, but God also wants us to pray collectively (Acts 2:42; 4:23-24, 31; 12:5; see 1 Cor. 14:15-17 where public prayer ought to be edifying for others). In prayer, we give thanks and praise to God, as well as pray for needs. In doing this properly, we are worshiping and honoring God.

They sang spiritual songs. We sing individually (Acts 16:25; Jas. 5:13), but there is great edification and strength in collective singing (Eph. 5:19-20; Col. 3:16-17). In singing, we edify each other, but we also "offer up a sacrifice of praise to God" (Heb. 13:15). The stress is on the individual's heart ("making melody with your heart"). If the heart is not right, then we "draw near" with our mouths, but our hearts are far from Him resulting in vain worship (Matt. 15:7-9). A later discussion considers the use of mechanical instruments of music in worship. Stress is never put on the entertainment value of music in worship. Though we encourage one another, God is ultimately our audience, and our hearts are His instruments of praise.

They taught God's message. The disciples taught and edified one another by studying God's will in the assembly (Acts 20:7; 1 Cor. 14). Letters written to churches were to be read to the group (Col. 4:16; 1 Tim. 4:13; Rev. 2-3). Does this constitute "worship"? Praise is included in much of what is read and taught from Scripture. While teaching others is not technically the same as direct praise to God, teaching truth does glorify and honor God because it is "good and acceptable in the sight of God" (1 Tim. 2:3). Whether some technically consider this worship or not, teaching is an assembly activity that glorifies God, and in that sense may be consdiered a form of worship.

They contributed funds to the work and encouraged carrying out the work. Some deny that giving is "worship," but consider the fact that, in our giving, we are honoring God and making it possible for the church to carry out its God-given task. Giving is one aspect of sharing, and sharing is offering up a sacrifice to God with which He is pleased (Heb. 13:16). 1 Corinthians 16:1-3 shows a collection being taken up for needy saints on the first day of the week, strengthening the point that the first day of the week was a regular time that Christians met.

How may we sum up guiding principles in our worship? 1) Since Jesus is King, we ought to be concerned with doing His will, according to His truth (John 8:31-32). 2) Each person should be concerned with worshiping God from the heart (cf. 1 Cor. 11:28; Matt. 15:7-9). 3) Worship should be edifying (1 Cor. 14). Though in a context of spiritual gifts, 1 Corinthians 14 shows principles of collective worship. Paul argues that whatever is done needs to be for the edification of the church (vv. 3, 12). If something did not edify the group, then it should not have been done in a group context. This principle applies to our activities. 4) Worship should be done decently and orderly. The Corinthians had a problem with people speaking out of order, with too many speaking, and with general confusion in the assembly. This violated God's will. "But all things must be done properly and in an orderly manner" (1 Cor. 14:40). While there is no specified chronological order for the activities, we must proceed in an orderly manner.

What about Incidental Matters?

There is a difference between something that is *purposed* and an *incidental* occurrence. "Incidental," means that something occurs as a casual accompaniment to something else that is purposed and planned. Our purpose is to come together to worship and praise God, as well as to edify and strengthen one another. In this context, incidentals happen. For example, while our purpose is not to be a social club or come together for mere social reasons, people do socialize when together. This is incidental to the purpose, but that doesn't mean it is unimportant. However, if we take this and turn it into our main purpose, then we have missed the point of our gathering. The greeting with a kiss (Rom. 16:16) was not the purpose for gathering, but was an incidental matter of custom that was to be guided by holiness.

What about announcements? In the context of a family meeting in order to encourage and edify, it is expedient to learn of the needs of others and to greet people in an orderly fashion. As members of the body trying to rejoice, weep, and care for each other, we need an expedient way of communicating these things (1 Cor. 12:26; Rom. 12:15). Public announcements are one way of doing this.

How does the building fit in? There is nothing inherently holy about a building. However, if the building was purchased with funds set aside for the work of God, then we need to be careful not to abuse that. There is a difference between allowing Boy Scout meetings and having Bible studies. What would limit the purposed use of the building is the authority by which it was built (an expedient meeting place in order to carry out the command to assemble and perform God's work). While it is generally authorized, it certainly can be abused.

Conclusion

Collective worship to God is a significant part of our lives as Christians. We need to make sure it is done properly, according to God's will and with proper hearts. We should avail ourselves of these opportunities.

Discussion Questions

1. Why is worship not confined only to a time or place?

2. What is true worship dependent upon and why?

3. Define worship. What does this tell us about how we should be approaching God?

4. How does Hebrews 9:1 inform us about worship under the Law?

5. Of what should we be careful in speaking about "acts of worship"?

6. Consider each of the areas discussed in which the assembly is engaged. What are the biblical reasons for doing these things? How do they honor and glorify God?

7. What overarching principles guide our activities in the assembly?

8. Why distinguish between a purpose and an incidental?

Grace, Love, and Authority

The announcement of salvation coincides with the message, "Your God reigns" (Isa. 52:7). Christians recognize that salvation comes by the grace of God through faith (Eph 2:8-10). With this comes the recognition of God's authority to offer grace. An offer of grace from one who has no authority would be worthless. Grace is meaningful because the One who offers that grace reigns. Only one with the power to heal can offer to heal.

We are not under Law but under grace (Rom 6:15). While there are debates over the nature of grace and works, this is more about understanding the relationship between grace and the authority of God. Because salvation to God's glory is our desire, thinking about grace and its connection to God's authority is fitting.

Grace and Covenant

God offers a covenant relationship in which He is merciful toward iniquities (Heb. 8:12). The only way that anyone can be in a covenant relationship with God is because of His grace (favor). We don't deserve mercy or forgiveness. Without His willingness to forgive, no amount of desire or action could earn it. Forgiveness cannot happen on our authority, but only on His, which is why we need to see this integral connection between grace and authority.

By recognizing God's grace, we confess that He is in charge of the relationship. We are not co-equals with God in a bilateral covenant. We cannot negotiate the terms of the contract (like two kings might do). In this covenant, He alone is King. We either submit ourselves to Him and His grace or we attempt to enthrone ourselves and thereby deny His grace. He is the beneficent King who willingly lavishes His grace upon us (Eph. 1:7-8). As the lesser is blessed by the greater (Heb. 7:7), so the lesser (us) is blessed by the grace of the Greatest of all.

The importance of this for our understanding of authority should be considered. People may think that grace allows freedom to do as we wish, as if grace is divorced from authority. If we are free in Christ because of His grace and mercy, then doesn't that mean we may do what we want? That is not a biblical view of grace. Rather, by recognizing His grace, we confess His absolute authority and right to command. By submitting to grace, we submit to His authority. Obedience to His expressed will recognizes that He sets the terms of the covenant, not us. Grace has never been a license to sin or to ignore God's will (see Rom. 6:1-2 and Jude 4).

This does not mean that we are under Law by which we may earn salvation. It does mean that grace is God's prerogative, and if we are going to be recipients of it, it will be on His terms, not ours. We bring to the table of the King our faith, which is a trusting, obedient submission to His will. We do not bring our own authority to the relationship, and we can make no demands on God. We might add things that we like and make us feel good, but it is a breach of our role in the covenant of God to extend our authority to the same level as His. Without His will, we have no warrant or right just to do whatever, for then we are working from our own authority, and this is a denial of His grace.

God's grace should keep us from thinking of God as some tyrant who just wants to squeeze people under his thumb. He is authoritative, but He is not tyrannical. We live under a marvelous covenant of grace and mercy. Even so, the Provider of the grace maintains all the power. Only when we keep our proper place under Him can we claim to be under this covenant of grace.

Some might think there is a conflict between grace and authority, like trying to put grace together with some form of meritorious law-keeping and self-righteousness. Nothing could be further from the truth. There is no grace unless the One offering that grace has the authority to give it. Since the terms of this covenant are His, by His grace, then we cannot have a proper view of grace without also seeing His authority. Grace teaches us to deny ungodliness, to live soberly and righteously, to look for the Lord's appearing, and to be zealous for the good works He gives for us to do (Titus 2:11-14). This exhortation is followed up with this: "These things speak and exhort and reprove with all authority" (vs. 15).

Authority with Grace

The only way God could, in His sovereignty, offer grace is if He has the authority to do so, and He does (Isa. 52:7). Anyone can say, "I'm giving you grace," or "I forgive you of your sins," but without the authority to enact grace, such a claim would be empty. God can extend His offer because He has the inherent authority to do so. Grace and authority are linked together in such a way that there could be no grace without God's absolute authority to offer it. This was one of the lessons of Mark 2:1-12. Jesus forgave the man's sins, then demonstrated His authority to do so. "But so that you may know that the Son of Man has authority on earth to forgive sins..." Authority and grace (e.g., forgiveness) go together.

One way we can learn to better appreciate God's grace is by continually recognizing His authority in everything. How so? First, recognizing the reliance upon God's grace admits our own failures and need for salvation. If we don't see the horror of sin and its consequences, then we will not see our need to rely upon God for forgiveness. A reliance upon grace is a reliance upon the power of God for that grace. If we rely upon our own authority rather than God's, then we are not living with trust in God's grace. If we don't recognize God's authority, then we will be relying on our own authority, and when we rely on our own authority, we negate grace because we are relying upon a self-appointed version of law.

When we act without God's authority, we are acting on our own (or another's) authority. This makes the work our own, not God's. Doing our own works and failing to submit to God and His works, we have fallen into our own system of justification. This is spoken against strongly in Scripture. For example, the concept of boasting for our own works is set over against God's grace and what He has done for us. Paul makes this point: "God has chosen the foolish things of the world to shame the wise, and God has chosen the weak things of the world to shame the things which are strong, and the base things of the world and the despised God has chosen, the things that are not, so that He may nullify the things that are, so that no man may boast before God. But by His doing you are in Christ Jesus, who became to us wisdom from God, and righteousness and sanctification, and redemption, so that, just as it is written, 'Let him who boasts, boast in the Lord.'" (1 Cor. 1:27-31)

God's authority is absolute. He did what He did to bring us to Him (1 Pet. 3:18), and His actions negate our ability to boast in our works precisely because we are not in a position to act on our own authority. Grace does not give permission to act outside of God's will (cf. Rom. 6:1-2; Jude 4). The irony is that the more we act on our own authority, the less we are respecting the grace of God. Authority and grace work together. If we respect God's authority, we will appreciate His grace all the more.

Love and Authority

Just as grace is tied to God's authority, so is love. Lack of love is manifested in selfishness. Love does not "seek its own" (1 Cor. 13:5, NASB), does not "insist on its own way" (ESV), is not "self-seeking" (NIV). When people push back against God's authority because they think they have a better way, a more loving way, they are not showing love. There is great irony in this. Culture tells us that we need to love more and to support all love between others. At the heart of this push is an attitude based on selfish ambition and the wisdom of the world. This is the same source where we will find bitterness, disorder, and every vile practice (Jas. 3:13-18). Worldly, cultural wisdom and understanding is not based on love because it seeks its own will and insists on its own way. Likewise, if we push against God's authority as Christians, seeking to run things our own way, putting our own desires and ambitions above others, ignoring what Scripture teaches, then we have failed to love. Putting a stamp of love on our own will only escalates the deception.

Love and authority go hand in hand. If we love God, we will submit to His authority because love does not seek its own will. If love is meaningful to us, so will God's authority be meaningful. We must not fool ourselves into thinking that, for the sake of love, we can compromise God's will. Jesus said, "If you love Me, you will keep My commandments" (John 14:15). Seek love, and in seeking love, seek after God's will instead of insisting on our own way.

"Love God" is the greatest commandment (Matt. 22:36-40). In the very context of that command (Deut. 6:4), Israel was told to fear God and keep His commandments. Loving Him and submitting to His will work together. We must show Him the respect He deserves, and to do so His way. Failure to respect this connection between love and authority results in love becoming a selfish excuse for doing what we want. The greatest command includes respecting everything about who God is, His sovereignty, and His will.

Conclusion

God's grace should humble us and cause us to see that it is only by His power and will that salvation is possible. "Your God reigns" is alongside the announcement of salvation (Isa. 52:7). Our King desires to lavish His grace and love upon us (Eph. 1:7-8), and knowing that He is the only One with that authority should comfort us. In return, let us seek to live by His grace and demonstrate our love for Him (Titus 2:11-14).

Discussion Questions

1. How is "Your God reigns" tied to salvation (Isa. 52:7)?

2. Why is God's authority vital when it comes to forgiveness?

3. How is a recognition of God's grace also a recognition of His authority?

4. How is acting on our own authority actually a denial of God's grace?

5. What does grace teach us to do (Titus 2:11-14)? Why is this so important?

6. How does Mark 2:1-12 show the connection of God's grace to His authority?

7. How do love and authority work together?

8. How should both love and grace keep us in humble submission to God and His will?

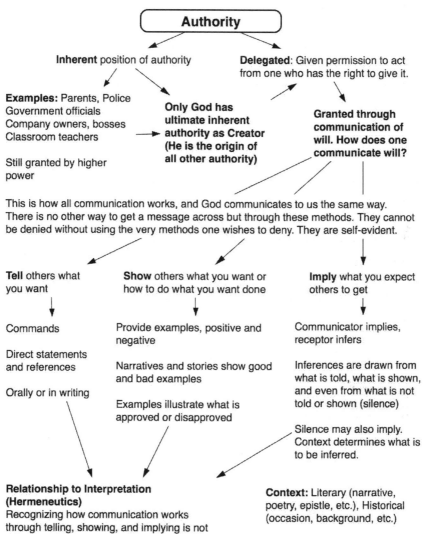

Authority

Inherent position of authority

Delegated: Given permission to act from one who has the right to give it.

Examples: Parents, Police Government officials Company owners, bosses Classroom teachers

Still granted by higher power

Only God has ultimate inherent authority as Creator (He is the origin of all other authority)

Granted through communication of will. How does one communicate will?

This is how all communication works, and God communicates to us the same way. There is no other way to get a message across but through these methods. They cannot be denied without using the very methods one wishes to deny. They are self-evident.

Tell others what you want

Show others what you want or how to do what you want done

Imply what you expect others to get

Commands

Direct statements and references

Orally or in writing

Provide examples, positive and negative

Narratives and stories show good and bad examples

Examples illustrate what is approved or disapproved

Communicator implies, receptor infers

Inferences are drawn from what is told, what is shown, and even from what is not told or shown (silence)

Silence may also imply. Context determines what is to be inferred.

Relationship to Interpretation (Hermeneutics)
Recognizing how communication works through telling, showing, and implying is not itself a method of interpretation (hermeneutic). Rather, what is told, shown, and implied comprise the raw material that is to be interpreted, understood, and applied. From here, other issues must be considered:

Doy Moyer

Context: Literary (narrative, poetry, epistle, etc.), Historical (occasion, background, etc.)

Who? What? When? etc. What does the text mean? How does it apply to our circumstances?

The communication process furnishes the beginning point of authority. Understanding exactly what it means and how it is to be applied is the role of hermeneutics.

Part 2

Essays on Biblical Authority

Specific or General

In discussions of biblical authority, it is not uncommon for a conversation to zero in on the question of specifics. One might argue the need for biblical authority, and another might then reply with questions like these:

- Where is the authority for a church building?
- Where is the authority for song books?
- Where is the authority for a song leader?
- Where is the authority for multiple cups for the Lord's Supper?

None of these answers are specified in Scripture, so on what grounds can we say they are authorized by Scripture? Sometimes those questions are legitimately coming from those who really desire the information and haven't understood. At other times, however, those who bring up questions like this are actually making an argument against the need for biblical authority in all that we do. The implied argument is this:

1. Since we don't have authority for church buildings and song books, then your argument for the need for authority either 1) shows that you are wrong, or 2) shows that you are being hypocritical.

2. Since we obviously don't have authority for everything (like buildings and song books), then our "method of establishing authority" is erroneous.

Though it sounds like a serious strike against authority, those who use this point as an argument misunderstand the basic nature of authority, primarily because they are not being consistent with the way communication works in every facet of life. Here, then, is the question: must everything we do be specified in order to be authorized?

The short answer is "no." The question is, on what basis can we argue that we must have authority on the one hand, but we don't always need specified statements on the other hand? How can something be authorized if it is not specified?

Must Everything Be Specified to Be Authorized?

The answer to this question goes back to the fundamentals of logic and communication. By doing this, we can avoid making arbitrary rules about authority that fit what we like, and instead we can be grounded in the actual communication process that functions logically everywhere. In other words, this is not just some arbitrary biblical rule we are making up, but rather it is how communication works in all areas and we are recognizing its function in biblical application. The beauty of this is that we already know how it works.

Think about the communication process. We have argued that we make our wills known to others by telling them what we want, showing them what we want, and implying what we expect them to understand. Virtually all telling and showing imply other factors that are not specified. For example, if I told my son to take out the garbage, without any further statements, I am implying that he can choose how to do that. Though I didn't specify every action involved (walk over to the cabinet, open the cabinet door where the trash is, pull the trash out, tie the garbage bag, pull it out of the can, walk to the outside door, open it with your hand, go to the outside garbage cans, open the lid of the one on the right, drop the bag into the big can … you get the idea!), I implied that as long as he does what I asked, he has some freedom in carrying out the task. I don't need to specify every single action in order to make my will known, and he has some freedom in carrying out my will. Which door he goes out, which hand he uses to open the door, how long he takes to do it, whether he uses a hand truck, etc. are all part of the choices he makes along the way. Without further specifications, these choices were all permitted by the simple order to take out the garbage. This process is so native to our communications with each other that we rarely have to think about it. We naturally understand how this works ... until we get to Scripture.

This principle falls under the category of what we think of as general authority. Something can be generally authorized by a more specific statement. If I tell my daughter, "Go buy some bread," there are both specific and general indicators. If that is all I said, then there are several actions that are permissible. She may "go" any number of ways: walk, ride a bike, drive a car, etc. She might even be able to purchase a couple of ways: use cash, swipe a debit card, etc. That would depend on what she had or what I give her. She might buy any number of types of bread: wheat, white, sourdough, rye, etc. On the other hand, the situation may imply that I expect a certain type of bread. We might have just run out of wheat bread for sandwiches, and the circumstances show that I am implying that this is what I want her to buy. Even then, when she goes to the store, since I didn't specify the brand name, she is free to pick up whatever she wishes ... unless, of course, we always only buy one brand and she already knows this. Context is the determiner.

When we communicate, there are many factors that need consideration. What we bring to the table as communicators, and what the recipient brings to the table need to be factored into the process. Further, the context under which the communication occurred must be considered. Most of this we subconsciously accept and we don't typically need it spelled out. We already know how it works.

When Scripture commands that we go teach and preach, the general entails the specific ways in which we can fulfill these commands. Whether we walk, ride, fly, or drive, we are still going. The fact that the Lord did not specify this part leaves us open to any number of ways of going. When we know it is the Lord's will that Christians meet together on the first day of the week, a variety of places to meet are included in fulfilling this. The general nature of God's expressed will allows for the variety of options, and we need to choose wisely (or, as is sometimes said, do what is most expedient for the group).

Specifics, Generalities, and Freedom

We must be mindful of another important principle that we learn from the communication process: the more specific something is, the less freedom we have in our interaction with it; conversely the more general something is, the more freedom we have.

This is not an arbitrary rule for Bible authority, but it is a principle of the communication process. We often disambiguate to make our intentions clear. If I ask my wife to buy me a red pen for grading papers, I surely don't mean to get me a blue one or a black one. Red is specific enough to rule out the other colors for my purposes. On the other hand, if I just asked for any pen, it is general enough to allow for all colors as long as it is a pen. The principle is fundamental and logical, and we do this regularly.

The principle works the same in biblical communication. In the Hebrew Scriptures, we find the principle at work. For example:

1. "Gopher wood" was more specific than just any "wood" (Gen. 6:14).
2. "Levites" was more specific than "people" in the service of the tabernacle (Num. 1:49-50).
3. The family of Aaron is more specific than "Levites" for priests (Exod. 28; Num. 16-17).
4. The specifics of the tabernacle were clear and didn't allow

for much variety (Exod. 25:9, 40; Heb. 8:5); David spoke of the "details of the pattern" of the Temple that Solomon would build (1 Chron. 28:19).

In the New Testament, we find the same principle.

1. There are many ways to sing, but "sing" is more specific than a general "make music," and what the passages authorize is singing (Eph. 5:19).
2. "Bread" is more specific than the more generic "food" (1 Cor. 11:23).
3. "Fruit of the vine" is more specific than "drink" (Matt. 26:29).
4. "Baptize" is more specific than "get wet" (Matt. 28:18-20)
5. "Go" is general enough to allow for a variety of ways to go (Matt. 28:19).
6. Coming together as a church requires a place (1 Cor. 11:18), but with no specific place commanded (cf. John 4:21-24), there is freedom to choose what will work best for the group.

Since not everything must be specified to be authorized, does this mean that we are free to do whatever we want to?

General authority does not equate to "whatever we want." The King is still in charge. If the command is general, we must still obey the command within boundaries and in the categories God gives. Going back to the store with my daughter, I might be general in asking her to buy bread, but she must still buy bread instead of whatever else she wanted. Even if I said, "Buy whatever food you think we might like for dinner," she still needs to come home with food. The given categories need to be observed.

A general order allows for more variety in carrying it out, but variety does not mean fundamentally changing what the general order expresses. If I ask for a writing instrument, then a pen or pencil will work, but if someone hands me a rock to write with, the point will have been missed.

Biblical examples show that we cannot legitimately use generalities to do what violates God's expressed will:

1. The new cart for the ark of the covenant (2 Sam. 6) violated what God said about the Levites carrying the ark.
2. Uzziah (2 Chron. 26:16-21) violated God's order for doing the work of the priesthood.
3. Nadab and Abihu offered a strange fire that God did not command (Lev. 10:1-2).

Not everything needs to be specified in order to be authorized. Therefore, when some argue that the authority argument insists that everything must be specified, they are misunderstanding the nature of the argument, if not the process of communication. Authority is grounded in fundamental logic and communication. Such communication includes the way we both specify and generalize our desires. God has communicated with us in the same way. Since we already know how it works, we are simply making the application to the communication that comes from Scripture.

General and Specific Categories in Communication

One of the reasons we take the position on authority that we do is because of the way communication normally works. As a follow-up to the previous question, "Must Everything be Specified to be Authorized?" we want to explore further the ways that specific and general statements operate in normal communication (and they often work without us even having to examine it this way; we typically just get it). Some of this may seem a bit too technical, but this may be due partly to the fact that we usually do not spell this process out; we just accept and understand it in normal communication. Nevertheless, for some reason, when we come to the Bible we might discard ordinary communication processes in favor of what we desire (then claim we are doing it out of love or from the heart). Yet, if God has expressed His will, and if we love Him, then we need to be concerned about how His will is actually communicated to us. Thus, while we wouldn't normally go into this kind of explanation for daily communication, we do it in order to show better why we talk about general and specific authority.

To better understand the nature of general and specific authority in biblical context, we wish to note some important aspects of standard logic first. In the following, "general" is essentially the same as "universal," and "specific" is essentially the same as "particular."

All propositions fit one of the following patterns (see Kreeft 148):

1. Universal Affirmative: all humans are mortal.
2. Universal Negative: no birds are cows.
3. Particular Affirmative: some humans are male.
4. Particular Negative: some animals are not dogs.

In the universal statement, the universal is the broad category. For example, in "all humans are mortal," "human" is the broad category that encompasses both male and female and every particular person. However, it would not necessarily be true (and it isn't) that all mortal entities are human. We cannot just flip the subject and predicate around in this case and have an equal statement. At the same time, though male and female both fit into the category of human, male and female are not identical; there are more particular categories within the broader category (and we can get even more particular if we specify individual males and females, etc.).

If we wanted a visual of this, think of circles within circles: the outer circle has the broad category (Mortal Entities); smaller, separated circles within this have subcategories (animals, humans); within the animal circle would be further specific circles (dogs, cats, cows); within the human circle would be gender circles (male, female); within the male and female circles might be specific people. The further into the circles we go, the more specific it gets, and the more specific it gets, fewer options are available.

Though particulars may share the same category, they are not identical to each other and should not be equated (else they lose their particularities). For example, within the bird category would fit the particulars of chicken, geese, sparrows, ravens, turkeys, and eagles. However, though all birds, they are not to be equated with each other (a sparrow is not a bald eagle). Blurring these distinctions would be fallacious.

If I said that I wanted something to write with, then any kind of writing instrument would work unless the context would show otherwise (pen, including all types of pens and colors, pencils, including mechanical and regular, medium and fine point, etc.). However, if I said that I wanted a red, felt-tipped, fine point pen, then only that specific type of pen would do. I could even specify the brand if I thought it mattered, and that would mean only that brand would fit my request, unless I indicate otherwise.

Likewise, if I said that I just wanted some food, pretty much any type of food would do (unless I specifically denied certain types like liver or sweets, or the context showed otherwise). However, if I said that what I wanted is a T-Bone steak with a baked potato, now I've been particular enough to rule out anything that is not what is specified. If I order this at a restaurant and they bring me spaghetti instead, that would not serve as an equal substitute for the order, even though it is food (and might, under other circumstances, be what I want). I would tell the waiter, "that's not what I ordered." Would that be unreasonable? Would that not be the normal response?

When we speak of animals in general, we include in that category dogs, cats, apes, deer, and all other animals. If we speak of dogs, however, we are not talking about cats. The general includes all the specifics of the category, but the specifics do not automatically include each other, even though in the same category.

Examples like these can be multiplied, and we use as many as we do in order to be clear about the way general and specific categories function in communication. When we specify something, we expect that it be respected. We do this continually, and we consider it to be reasonable. How, then, does this work with biblical authority?

The question is, why would it work any differently in understanding God's revealed will? We have been arguing all along that issues in biblical authority are rooted in the fundamentals of logic and communication. The point of the above is to show that we are not making arbitrary rules when it comes to biblical authority, but are, rather, applying fundamental logic and communication principles that we understand in every other area of life. As with the given illustrations, general orders include the specifics that fall under the general category, but specified orders do not include everything in the general category. If only a very general order is given, then all the specifics within that order are permissible; therefore something can be authorized even though not specified. However, the more specified the order, the fewer the options. Red is not blue, dogs are not cats, and singing is not the same as instrumental music.

For example, in the Lord's Supper instructions, we have been shown particulars (bread and fruit of the vine, Matt 26:26-29; 1 Cor 11:23-25). Had the information simply been "food," then we would have been free to operate within the general category of food and choose what we wish for the Lord's Supper. However, the particulars are given, and we are not free to substitute whatever we wish just because we like something else. If we want to use something else, then we need to find where something else is indicated by God. For the Lord's Supper, ham is not to be equated with the bread (even though it shares the food category), and soda cannot be equated with the fruit of the vine (even though it shares the drink category). Food and drink are the categories, but since the particulars are given, we do well to stay with those particulars and not try to substitute other particulars according to our liking.

In recognizing these principles, we are not making arbitrary rules. We are simply pointing out how communication operates in everyday usage, then making that same application to our biblical understanding. Communication is universal, and we cannot ignore the way it works just because our desires are otherwise. Why would we recognize these principles in all other fields but apply different rules when we come to Scripture? That would be a very arbitrary form of interpretation. We seek for consistency, and thus apply this principle of the general and specified authority.

If we love the Lord, we will keep His will (cf. John 14:15). His will is expressed through language, and language means something purposeful. It is because we love the Lord that we want to listen carefully to how He has communicated His will to us.

Patterns

Is God a God of patterns or of randomness? A pattern is a "form or model proposed for imitation," an "exemplar." It is "something designed or used as a model for making things." An "exemplar" is "an admired person or thing that is considered an example that deserves to be copied." It is "an ideal model" of something (Miriam-Webster).

Some argue that there are no patterns in Scripture for matters like worship, the body of Christ, or even salvation. What is the alternative? A lack of patterns means randomness. Even the dictionary (.com) defines randomness as "proceeding, made, or occurring without definite aim, reason, or pattern..." or "lacking a definite plan, purpose, or pattern" (*Mirriam-Webster*). When there are no patterns, all is random, and there is no definite aim. There is no particular plan to follow, and this says something about purpose.

Is this what people want to say about God's will under Christ? Is Christianity random, aimless, or without purpose? Is worship meant to be random? If there are no patterns, what are we supposed to do? What plan do we follow? What purpose do we espouse? Will those who deny patterns tell us? Will they be the makers of new patterns? A religion without a pattern is a religion of chaos, and chaos is not what the Lord is about. Let's take another look at this concept of patterns in Scripture.

God and Patterns

Typology alone (repetition of patterns) shows that God is a God of patterns. Without even going through a process of trying to "establish" authority, we can see how God shows through His overall record that He is a God of repeating patterns. This is evident right from the beginning when God made a pattern for creation that He later replicated in the work week of Israel. The Sabbath was a pattern that they were to follow (Ex 20:11). Patterns are found in other items like the tabernacle, the priesthood, and the sacrificial system. Patterns are an integral part of Scripture.

There is also a strong pattern of God's will for obedience throughout Scripture. The Law was clear. God's people were to follow it, not turn from it to the right or left, and diligently obey it (Joshua 1). Passage after passage shows this.

Deuteronomy 6 shows that the people were to keep diligently the commands "that it may be well with you." They were to "listen and be careful" (see vv 1-3). Yet, notice that it is in this very same context where the greatest commandment of all is given: "You shall love the Lord your God with all your heart and with all your soul and with all your might. These words, which I am commanding you today, shall be on your heart..." (vv. 5-6).

There is no inherent conflict between loving God with all the heart and diligently being careful to obey. The two are so intertwined that one cannot love God without being careful to obey. Jesus said, "If you love Me, you will keep my commandments" (John 14:15). Those who find a problem in this have misunderstood either what obedience to God is about, or what it means to love Him, or both.

Some may try to pit careful adherence to obedience over against loving God. Arguing as if the Old Covenant was about strict obedience while loving God with the all the heart is what living for Jesus is all about, some fail to connect the fact that such strict obedience under the Old Covenant was closely tied to their need to love God.

Never has there been a time when God did not want or expect His people to love Him with all their hearts. Never has God accepted cold, rote ritual in lieu of loving Him. God has always wanted people to do justice, love kindness, and walk humbly with Him (Micah 6:8), and never has any of this contradicted the need to be careful in diligently obeying Him.

Christ did not come to free us from patterns of obedience. He came to free us from the patterns of sin. He didn't change the context or the concepts inherently involved in loving God with all the heart. He strengthened them.

When Israel was at Sinai, God was explicit about their need to follow patterns, particularly in building the tabernacle. "According to all that I am going to show you, as the pattern of the tabernacle and the pattern of all its furniture, just so you shall construct it" (Ex 25:9). "See that you make them after the pattern for them, which was shown to you on the mountain" (Exod. 25:40; see Heb. 8:5). "… according to the pattern which the Lord had shown Moses, so he made the lampstand" (Num. 8:4).

Stephen pointed this out in his recounting of their history: "Our fathers had the tabernacle of testimony in the wilderness, just as He who spoke to Moses directed him to make it according to the pattern which he had seen" (Acts 7:44). The Hebrews writer also pointed to these patterns (Heb. 8:5). God is a God of patterns!

Free from Patterns in Christ?

Weren't these patterns just part of the old system? Aren't we free in Christ? Hasn't He freed us from legal codes, so that now we just need to show love, kindness, and mercy? Strict "patternism" has been done away with, so God is no longer concerned with following patterns, is He? Where, in the New Covenant Scriptures, is the idea that we are free from patterns ever taught? Not by Jesus. Not by Paul or Peter. If God meant to abandon patterns under Christ, we have no indication of it by any normal means of communication. We aren't told, shown, or given any implications whatsoever about being free of all patterns.

Why do we have the Old Covenant Scriptures? God did not intend for these passages to disappear under Christ. Jesus came to fulfill, not destroy (Matt 5:17). Fulfillment did not mean that suddenly this God of patterns is no longer such a God and that He wants to leave it up to the people to do what they feel is good in serving and worshipping Him. God has not changed. He defines love for us, and He wants our faithfulness no less than He did from those under the Old Covenant. The Hebrews writer even makes an *a fortiori* argument (argument from a stronger reason — if A, then how much more B?). If God expected faithfulness under Moses, how much more under Christ?

"Anyone who has set aside the Law of Moses dies without mercy on the testimony of two or three witnesses. How much severer punishment do you think he will deserve who has trampled under foot the Son of God, and has regarded as unclean the blood of the covenant by which he was sanctified, and has insulted the Spirit of grace?" (Heb 10:28-29)

To disregard what God commands under Christ is to insult Christ and the "Spirit of grace." The very fact that Jesus is the fulfillment of the old strengthens the case for patterns. He is the fulfillment of God's patterns. Those patterns don't unravel in Christ; they are a vital part of who He is. It was in the tabernacle that God was so specific about His patterns. Jesus is that tabernacle; He is the very presence of God, dwelling (tenting) among His people (John 1:1, 14).

The Old Covenant Scriptures were given for our benefit. We are not under its stipulations, but we are under its advisement.

"As to this salvation, the prophets who prophesied of the grace that would come to you made careful searches and inquiries, seeking to know what person or time the Spirit of Christ within them was indicating as He predicted the sufferings of Christ and the glories to follow. It was revealed to them that they were not serving themselves, but you, in these things which now have been announced to you through those who preached the gospel to you by the Holy Spirit sent from heaven —things into which angels long to look" (1 Peter 1:10-12).

"For whatever was written in earlier times was written for our instruction, so that through perseverance and the encouragement of the Scriptures we might have hope" (Rom 15:4).

That which was written, whether through narrative, prophecy, poetry, or implicit typology are still given for our benefit. God establishes patterns throughout. To see how particular and meticulous God was about patterns in the Old, then to come to the New Covenant Scriptures and argue that there are no patterns at all, is to jump the fence of reason. God established patterns, but not to give them up and destroy them under Christ. Patterns show us a God who is concerned about details. He is a God who is orderly, not chaotic (cf. 1 Cor. 14:33).

Finally, patterns are an undeniable part of the New Covenant. We note the following Scriptures:

- "Brethren, join in following my example, and observe those who walk according to the pattern you have in us" (Phil. 3:17)
- "Now we command you, brethren, in the name of our Lord Jesus Christ, that you keep away from every brother who leads an unruly life and not according to the tradition which you received from us" (2 Thess. 3:6).
- "Now concerning the collection for the saints, as I directed the churches of Galatia, so do you also" (1 Cor 16:1).

- "That is why I sent you Timothy, my beloved and faithful child in the Lord, to remind you of my ways in Christ, as I teach them everywhere in every church" (1 Cor. 4:17).
- "Retain the standard (pattern) of sound words which you have heard from me, in the faith and love which are in Christ Jesus" (2 Tim. 1:13).

These, and many more, passages demonstrate a serious concern for detail, for doing things the way God orders, and for teaching that was done everywhere. This is not a random matter, but shows a God of patterns and order.

Much of the Old Covenant foreshadows the New (i.e., typology). The study of typology is a study of patterns (e.g., the creation pattern, the Exodus pattern, the tabernacle pattern, the sacrifice pattern). God is, indeed, a God of patterns. It's quite amazing. God has always cared about patterns, and they comprise the message of Scripture from beginning to end.

Biblical Depth and Beauty

Seeing patterns in Scripture can open our eyes to greater ideas and thoughts contained therein that we may have been missing. There are days when, during my Bible study, I think to myself, "Where have I been? Why didn't I see that before? How could I have been so blind here?"

There is a depth and beauty to Scripture that can easily be missed, depending on how we are reading it and what our goals are when we read. We might have a tendency to read the Bible in some strict linear fashion. We read from Genesis to Revelation and tell the story, and this is necessary. Yet how often do we read while failing to make connections between passages and concepts? We may see a flat-line story without seeing the layers of connections of ideas that are interwoven throughout. The Bible is not just a linear story. It is an interwoven tapestry filled with layers and webs of beautiful patterns. If a written text can be said to be 3-D, Scripture is that! We need to put our glasses on so we can see its depth leaping off the pages. It's there if we'll see it.

Scripture is filled with relationships of concepts. Patterns, types and antitypes, shadows and substance, are staples of understanding the importance of connections. For example, "For Christ our passover has been sacrificed" (1 Cor 5:7) is a beautiful statement of pattern and connection. The book of Hebrews is filled with it and cannot be understood without seeing this. The book of Revelation's connections back to the Old Testament are grand and exploding with meaning. The way that the New Testament quotes the Old Testament adds a depth that we might easily miss (e.g., "Out of Egypt I have called My Son," Matt 2:15); it is certainly a challenging study. Over and over, we find fulfillment of both prophecy and concept. The biblical story is told many ways and through many images, from the Garden, to the Exodus, the Temple, the holy city of Jerusalem and more, finding masterful fulfillment in Christ. There is a great joy of discovery when we see these connections and begin understanding the depth at which these connections are made. This is one reason why Bible study should never become cold, lifeless, or boring. If we are bored with Bible study, we haven't turned our minds on yet.

The beauty and depth of Scripture, including the patterns, is part of God's inspiration. Failing to see some of this depth is part of the reason, I am convinced, that people end up rejecting Scripture. People might take passages, read them flatly, and conclude some kind of contradiction or problem, when, in reality, they are missing the depth of what the passages are teaching because they draw hasty conclusions without putting much thought into it.

For example, many times I have seen critics of Scripture, in somewhat of a mocking tone, try to discount the Bible by making some flippant remark about how ridiculous it is to follow the Bible when it contains commands about not mixing fabrics together. If they know where the reference is, they seldom know anything about the context of the passage, the covenants, or the greater issues involved. They see a flat-line order that sounds silly on the surface, and they run with that impression.

"You are to keep My statutes. You shall not breed together two kinds of your cattle; you shall not sow your field with two kinds of seed, nor wear a garment upon you of two kinds of material mixed together." (Lev 19:19)

Reading it flatly, and without further consideration, one can think of how senseless this sounds. If we even read Leviticus, how often would we skim over a passage like this and just think, "That's weird, but, oh well, that's part of the Law"? We must think deeper. One of the points that is easily missed is that God was teaching an overall culture of holiness and pure-minded devotion. One of the ways that He got people to think about that was through physical and visible reminders, even in their daily, mundane activities. Through engaging in actions that forced their minds toward the ideas of cleanness, holiness, not mixing with the unholy, pagan people of the land, they would be more inclined to remember how important it was to remain faithful always. Not mixing materials was a daily reminder, even in the way they constructed and wore their clothes, to stay pure, unmixed with sin, and faithful to God. It would be like our putting Bible sticky notes on mirrors and refrigerators as reminders that no matter where we are or what we are doing, we are to be holy and pure. Being a child of God encompasses all areas of life, including how business is conducted, how work is done, and how we do our mundane activities. There may even be more, but the point is that a passage like this, flatly read, is boring and silly. Seen in its greater context and message, it is brilliantly reminding God's people how overarching holiness was to be in their lives. It wasn't so much about the fabric as much as it was about the lesson derived from the process and the action. I even find it intriguing that this comes on the heels the second-greatest commandment.

Of course, there are cautions. We don't want to overdo it. One does not have to be some super intellect to study and understand. Nor should we try to see phantom connections or start allegorizing everything. Not at all. Scripture makes the connections, shows the contexts, and leads us to draw the conclusions. Our task is to see them, not to invent things for the sake of novelty.

To connect this back to authority, we should see that how we understand authority and how we interpret Scripture are interwoven. Understanding God's authority should be grounded in the big picture of Scripture, the patterns of Scripture, and the basic communication processes of which all are familiar. Studying Scripture has many facets, but at the bottom is still the fact that Scripture communicates God's mind.

Bible study is to be a careful undertaking, not a hasty effort at proof-texting that requires little thought or sound exegesis. Such hasty efforts lead not only to poor understanding and bad interpretation, they can lead to rejection of Scripture altogether. Flat-line Bible reading contributes to flat-line spirituality. If people are bored with Scripture, they'll be bored with their "religion."

Let's open our eyes and see the beauty and the depth of God's word, and prepare to be amazed!

"When one turns to the question of authority in religion the basic problem immediately arises: is there anything in religion which demands that a man think a certain way about religion and not another? Is there a man, a society, a principle, or a document which has the right to prescribe religious belief?

"Nothing could be more foolish in religion than the rejection of an authority which contained the truth of the living God; and nothing could be more tragic than the substitution of the voice of man for the voice of God." — Bernard Ramm (16)

Tradition!

Where does the teaching originate? Christians need to pay attention to the word of God "as a lamp shining in a dark place" (2 Pet 1:19). Why? Because "no prophecy of Scripture is a matter of one's own interpretation" (vs. 20). Scripture's origin is from God rather than men, "for no prophecy was ever made by an act of human will, but men moved by the Holy Spirit spoke from God."

2 Peter 2:1 follows as a contrast between what originated with God's will with what originates from men. The false teachers secretly introduce heresies, maligning the truth and exploiting people. They are "daring" and "self-willed" (vs. 10). The question of whether a teaching originates with God or men is not academic. It gets to the heart of whether or not we are seeking our own will or God's will.

Traditional Teaching

A tradition is something that is passed down, and all sound teaching is what has already been given, unless we are pulling new things out of nowhere. Speaking against "traditional," without further clarity, makes little sense, for if we are teaching what has never been taught, and if we cannot find biblical support for it, then something is wrong (see 2 Thess. 2:15).

It makes little sense in any universal context to fight all "tradition." What is traditional to some may depend upon where they were brought up and what was taught. For many, calling something "traditional" poisons the well by labeling something in a negative way, which makes people suspicious of it. This does not help further the discussion. Either a teaching finds its authority in Scripture or it doesn't. That's really what matters here.

Tradition and God's Word

Mark 7 records one of Jesus' confrontations with the Pharisees, who had seen Jesus' disciples eating with unwashed hands. The tradition was that they were to wash their hands very carefully before eating, and "there are many other things which they have received in order to observe, such as the washing of cups and pitchers and copper pots." They confronted Jesus: "Why do Your disciples not walk according to the tradition of the elders, but eat their bread with impure hands?" (vs. 5) Let's note:

1. Washing hands before eating is good practice; there was nothing inherently wrong here.
2. That Tradition is fine. Some traditions can be noteworthy and good.
3. However, the appeal of the Pharisees is the tradition. They did not ask about the disciples breaking the Law of God.

Jesus responded first by calling them hypocrites, second by quoting Isaiah 29, and third by showing how they were placing their traditions above God's commandments.

In Isaiah 29, Isaiah rebuked God's people for idolatry and apathy toward the covenant. Isaiah 1 rebuked Israel for merely going through the motions of offering sacrifices, but then committing all kinds of evil. Ironically, Isaiah does tell the people to wash themselves and make themselves clean (Isa 1:16), but his emphasis was not physical. "Remove the evil of your deeds from My sight." This was the way they were to clean themselves, and it is a far more important kind of washing than we can ever do with the hands. God says, "their reverence for Me consists of tradition learned by rote" (Isa. 29:13). They cared little for the Law. When Jesus called the Pharisees hypocrites, He was noting how they were neglecting the commandments of God for the sake of their traditions. They were chastising others for failing to keep a tradition while they were guilty of violating God's commands.

Traditions are a part of life. To one degree or another, all that we know is passed down. However, how we act about those traditions is another matter. We must distinguish between traditions that are commandments of God and those handed down otherwise. If we put man-made traditions on par with, or over, God's word, then we are guilty of hypocrisy. This is the point made in Isaiah 29:15-16.

Jesus illustrated how they had neglected the command to honor father and mother. They were more concerned about washing their hands than they were about caring for their parents. If we are not careful, we can fall into the same trap. Human traditions change, but what we receive from God's word will never change. Let's be careful to make that distinction. Even more, let's be careful to engage in God's will over our own. That is the the primary issue at stake.

Tradition as Error, Truth, and Choice

Traditions may come in at least these forms:

Error. A tradition can be passed down as an error. Jesus challenged this kind of tradition in Mark 7, where the Pharisees had violated God's Law with their "Corban" tradition. Wrong-headed traditions need to be challenged and overthrown. This is not to be done, however, based on mere preference or whim, but on truth. If a practice or teaching is erroneous, then truth needs to prevail, lest we find ourselves under Jesus' rebuke: "Why do you yourselves transgress the commandment of God for the sake of your tradition?" (Matt 15:3)

Truth. God expected His truth to be passed down through time, and this, too, is tradition, as Paul wrote: "So then, brethren, stand firm and hold to the traditions which you were taught, whether by word of mouth or by letter from us" (2 Thess 2:15). If we are teaching new doctrines that did not originate in Scripture, for the sake of doing non-traditional things, then we have conflated tradition as truth with tradition as error or choice. Tradition as truth should always be upheld and practiced, and failure to do so will put us out of line with God's revealed will.

Choice. By "choice," we mean that the tradition is neither necessary nor wrong. Not all traditions are necessary (#2). They might help facilitate the teaching of truth, and they might be reasonable expedients depending on the circumstances (e.g., meeting twice on Sundays or using song books), but they are not required. Neither are they wrong, but the danger is that we get used to doing something by choice and then confuse these traditions with truth itself. That is, if the tradition by choice is changed, we fight like it is the truth that is being compromised, when it is, instead, just choices we have made. On the other hand, some try to change tradition by choice and may take an approach that is offensive and disrespectful toward those who prefer the tradition to remain as is. There is no need to change such a tradition just for the sake of change, but neither is there a reason to hold on to it if the reason for changing it is warranted. People need to be reasonable, respectful, and open-minded in dealing with tradition as choice.

For clarity and unity, we must understand the differences between these types of tradition. Many divisions and problems can occur because we just label something "traditional" without further clarifying what we mean by it. Someone may fight against a "tradition as truth" while thinking it is "tradition as choice," or vice-versa, and problems ensue.

1. We should figure out where the tradition we are considering fits. Is it error? Is it truth? Or is it choice?

2. Then we can look at options: 1) reject it if it is error; 2) accept it

and practice it if it is truth; or 3) consider our options and weigh the effects if it is choice.

3. Divisive attitudes should never prevail, especially over tradition as choice.

Illustrated: Is it Old, New, or True?

Receiving and practicing the word of God is all about attitude. Truth is not determined by our feelings or preferences. Truth is objective, real, discoverable, and applicable. Truth must be based upon what Scripture teaches. Consider Acts 17.

1. There were those who refused to hear anything new (vv 1-9). Some Jews in Thessalonica did not want to hear about Jesus and the resurrection. They became jealous, accusing Paul and his companions of turning the world upside down. When we close our minds to hearing something new to us, we put ourselves in the same position as these who became upset at the gospel. For them, the resurrection was too new, too radical, too non-traditional. They wanted to protect the status quo, and this mentality did not bode well for them. Neither will it bode well for us. Protecting the status quo of tradition is pointless when it opposes truth.

2. There were those who only wanted to hear new things (vv 16-34). On these grounds some in Athens were willing to listen to Paul. However, many would only listen until that "new thing" demanded a change in their behavior as they were called upon to repent. Once the resurrection was brought into it, which demanded repentance, they began to sneer. "New things" have their limits, even for those who consider themselves tolerant. Sometimes those who pride themselves on being open-minded, liberal, and tolerant, will quickly close their minds when their worldview is seriously challenged. It is one thing philosophically to consider a different view; it is quite another matter when that position challenges one to make fundamental changes to comply with God's will. The gospel will not allow us to rest easy and comfortable with our position, no matter how open we are. There is no real value to being open-minded to new things when we shut ourselves off to truth.

3. There were noble-minded ones who wanted truth (vv 10-15). "Now these were more noble- minded than those in Thessalonica, for they received the word with great eagerness, examining the Scriptures daily to see whether these things were so" (vs. 11). They were not evaluating what they heard based on whether or not they ever heard something before. They weren't asking, "is it old?" or, "is it new?" They were asking, "is it true?" This is noble.

Tradition in itself is not the problem. We must learn to evaluate whether any tradition is based on truth, error, or choice. Truth stands on its own and is what we need eagerly to receive. "Examining the Scriptures daily" is the mark of those who seek truth. Let's choose the honorable path exemplified by the Bereans. Let's choose the way that God labels as noble-minded.

On Changing Traditions

If a tradition is wrong, then, of course, we must change it. If tradition is truth, then we must never change it. What about traditions of choice? Do we change something because there is a good reason to do so? If so, there shouldn't be any problems with this, and it could be very good. If it is well explained and a group agrees, it is their prerogative. Do we change something just for the sake of changing it? This may not be wrong, but there is a legitimate question as to why, and without explanation some would likely be confused. Maybe changing something once in a while is a good thing, but no one wants to be in the dark as to why things are suddenly different. I don't run into many who get upset for changing how many songs are sung before a prayer or whether the Lord's Supper comes a little earlier or later. Other changes might be a little more deserving of an explanation.

Here's the question: Do we change something just because we are bored with it? If so, there may be other issues to address. When traditions are perfectly acceptable (not in violation of what is right, and competently perform the task at hand), yet the ones practicing them feel tired, bored, and unexcited, the answer is not to change the tradition, but to change the heart. A bored heart will only momentarily be excited with a change in outward circumstances. A converted heart will not be deterred, no matter the circumstances. A bored heart will not finally be satisfied by changing the order of services, how many songs are sung, or whether the group meets once or twice on a Lord's day.

Again, this is not to say that a tradition by choice cannot be changed. However, the change ought to be for legitimate reasons rather than as a band aide for a heart that has lost its zeal. Just changing a tradition can become a smoke-screen for addressing the wrong issue and, ultimately, it changes nothing. Soon that heart will require more change in order to feed its need for external stimulation. Just as the eye is not satisfied with seeing, the ear with hearing (Eccl 1:8), or the one who loves money cannot be satisfied with money (5:10), so the bored heart cannot be satisfied with anything simple and traditional. More stimulation will always be needed. The heart wrapped up in new things is not the noble heart praised by God (cf. Acts 17:11), but is the one intent on its own glory and appeasement. Only something new will do (cf. Acts 17:21). Such a heart seeks its own will, all the while judging others for hypocrisy and mere traditionalism, not understanding that converted hearts can be happy with simplicity and proper tradition. Such is an attempt at self justification by bringing others down. Yet, as we are sometimes reminded, one's own light does not shine brighter by trying to diminish the lights of others.

Changing traditions carries a delicate balance. If a group is somewhat divided over changing a choice, shall we push ahead anyway when others are perfectly happy with how things are being done? Shall we change something to the hurt of others just because it is what we want to do and "who cares what others think"? Shall we change things if it causes divisions and factions, and will doing such be justified if we smugly appeal to our rights? Shall we be justified if we show that the "other side" is being obstinate about a choice? Shall we change things to prove some point about our rights? Even if we have rights, how far do we take them? How adamant are we over matters of choice? I realize that the "other side" can be just as stubborn, even to the hurt of a group. I know that one person who wants no change at all can demand that things be done his or her way, and this cannot be healthy. I know there are those who spy out liberties and make unreasonable demands. But this is not really what I'm talking about here. Let's look at our hearts to make sure we are not guilty of pushing our own rights and wills to the harm of a group out of personal boredom, and let's be careful in dealing with our brothers and sisters of all ages for whom Christ died.

Loving God is more important than appeasing our desire for something new. Loving others is more important than our rights. I have no problem with changing traditions of choice, but I want to know that there is a purpose to our actions (as part of a local group). If it is a matter of personal boredom and a need for new things, then at some point those outward changes will not be enough. Let's start with the heart. Let's work for unity. Above all, let's be committed to the Lord and His will.

On Keeping Tradition

Once again, traditions can be practiced as a matter of truth (2 Thess 2:15), error (Matt 15:3-9), or choice (not required, but not wrong). Still staying within the realm of traditions that are neither erroneous nor required, we not only want to think about why we would want to change a tradition (see On Changing Traditions), but also why we are intent on maintaining a tradition. Also, we should be clear that we can only address traditions such as we have in mind here at the local level. Every group has the liberty to work out their traditions by choice, and others should respect local group autonomy.

Here are some questions for thought:

1. Just as we don't want to change tradition without good reason, how safe and spiritually sound is it to merely keep a tradition without being able to articulate good reason for it? Do we do it just because that's the way it has always been done (which is not so likely if it is a tradition by choice)? Do we do it because we are convinced it is the best and most expedient choice for the group? Do we think about it at all?

2. Is it possible to keep a tradition to the detriment of a group? What if it is more expedient to change a tradition of choice for the sake of the group and one refuses to consider it? Is a tradition of choice worth dividing over? Are we willing to make a change if we know that the group believes it important to do so?

3. Is it possible that we are keeping the tradition out of pride and self will? Is it possible that we think as much or more of the tradition as we do Scripture? Have we asked ourselves why we are intent on a tradition? Have we examined the Scriptures often and recently, or do we just take it all for granted?

When a tradition is challenged or questioned (reasonably, not belligerently), how do we react? Are we defensive about it? Are we reasonable and willing to discuss what is best for the group in order to glorify God? Are we willingly reexamining what we are doing to make sure we are appropriately seeking to serve God and others? Are we really willing to make a change if there are good reasons to do so in our given situation? If not, what would that say about our true commitment. Are we more committed to God or to our own ways?

None of this is to suggest that a group must continually change traditions. Such would likely cause confusion, as change just for the sake of change can be a problem and indicate boredom more than real efforts to glorify God. Rather, this is to challenge us to be thinkers, knowing exactly what we are doing and why. God does not wish us to be mindless robots, but He wants us to engage the heart and the mind (even as the greatest commandment indicates).

If we mindlessly keep traditions of choice, how is this demonstrating love for God or others? If we get angry when such a tradition is questioned or brought up for consideration of change, how is this not putting the tradition on par with or even over God's word? Here is the problem we cannot afford. If we hold to a tradition of choice with the same force (maybe more) and vigor to which we would hold truth itself, then we have elevated our thinking to divine status. We cannot consistently chastise some for departing from the faith and going beyond Scripture when we are tenaciously protecting and defending a tradition of choice as if it is a sacred cow that cannot be touched. Such would amount to idolatry in its own right, which is why it is so important to think about all the actions we are taking in a group setting.

It is, therefore, vital that we properly distinguish tradition by truth from tradition by choice. The practice of the Lord's Supper is necessary; meeting a second time on Sunday is a choice. Edification by Scripture is required of God; the exact wording of a sign (assuming it does not convey an unbiblical concept) on a building is a choice (even the building itself or having a sign at all is a choice). Of course, a group must take care in this, for just as it is possible to elevate a tradition of choice to the status of divine command, so it is possible to demote divine command to the status of choice. Making what's optional necessary, and making what's necessary optional are both erroneous and puts our thinking over God's thinking. We must exercise great care.

Once we distinguish the types of tradition, we will be in a position to make wise choices within a congregational setting. Our goal, as always, is to glorify God and please Him. No tradition of choice is worth holding to the point of losing souls. Cling to the truth tenaciously; hold on loosely to traditions of choice that need occasional reevaluation. Each group will consider its circumstances and needs in order to make proper choices for the most effective way to glorify God in their community. Again, all of this is to be done within the boundaries of divine authority as revealed in Scripture.

Tradition is what has been passed down. There is tradition that we ought to be practicing, and tradition that we ought to avoid. The key is learning to identify the difference. Truth is the standard by which we measure it all. If we need to change it, then let's have the courage to conform to the truth and change. If we need to keep it, then let's be committed to doing that. If it's choice, then let's apply wisdom and maintain peace and unity among ourselves.

The Logic of Authority

Someone has to be in charge. It only makes sense. While we may dream of a society where there are few laws, just imagine having no laws. Take away all speed limits, all road rules, all laws dealing with lanes and directions, and where do you think that will get us? Without rules, authority, and the ability to back it up, society cannot long survive in any civilized fashion. Even Utopia had its rules that were punished upon violation. Read the book.

The same is true of other areas of life: school, business, and the home all require authority. Acting like no one is ever in charge is not a situation anyone can long stand. "Isn't anyone in charge here?" bellows the customer who can't seem to find answers to the most basic questions. "Can I talk to someone in authority? Can I see your manager?" There is always an expectation that someone is in charge, and we often recognize that going "to the top" is the only way to get something done. Again, it only makes sense. And we know it does. No further proof is needed.

Suppose, though, that people wish to reject the idea of authority altogether. Then where exactly will they turn? Themselves? Others? Are we really to believe that they will reject all authority? It's not even possible. The logic of authority is that there is no escaping it. Authority is basic because no one can avoid it. It is logically self-evident. Even if people try to avoid God's authority, they will still rely on another source for the authority by which they do anything, whether their own or another's. To contradict the point is self-defeating. DM

Instrumental Music

"Now even the first covenant had regulations of divine worship and the earthly sanctuary" (Heb. 9:1).

The purpose of God's People collectively and individually is to Glorify God (1 Pet. 2:9; Col. 3:16-17). A congregation assembles to offer praise and worship to God. The concern is offering worship that is acceptable to God (1 Pet. 2:5), and worship has long been prone to abuse. The primary question is, who regulates worship? (See Deut. 12:30-32; Col. 2:20-23; Matt. 15:3) The real concern, then, ought to be not what pleases us, but what pleases God. Herein is the primary reason for stressing biblical authority.

Please note that the issue addressed here is directly related to what a congregation does in its public assembly as worship to God. The question of the use of instruments in congregational worship has continued to be one of the more emotionally charged issues of today. Some will argue that it just doesn't matter, and some will charge those who oppose their use with being legalists. While emotions can run high on both sides of this issue, it is yet fair to explain why some of us continue to oppose their use in worship. This is not so much out of a desire to debate the subject as much as to provide reasons for a more well-informed discussion.

Also note that this is not just a modern "Church of Christ" issue, as if only churches of Christ began opposing instruments (see, for example, *Old Light on New Worship*, by John Price, a Baptist pastor who opposes instruments in worship; some of the arguments here will reflect some of what he wrote).

To begin, we offer here a synopsis that provides a few basic reasons why there are those who still argue against the use of mechanical instruments in the congregational worship of God. The arguments typically fit within the following:

Basic Arguments Against the Instrument

No Warrant. While the Old Testament shows their use by God's authority, the New Testament documents give no indication of God desiring instruments in congregational worship now. With no such indication of God's desire for instruments under the New Covenant, we are without warrant in using them, and those who do use them have the burden of proof to show such a warrant. The issue then revolves around how to understand God's silence on an issue. Some argue that silence is permissive, while others argue that silence gives no authority to act. There are many layers to these arguments, of course. The bottom line is that those who argue against instruments do so on the basis of authority. He is in charge of His worship, not us. God clearly desires singing (e.g., Eph 5:19), but gives no indication that He wants mechanical instruments added to the singing in worship. Since God was so specific about instruments under the Old Covenant, His silence on the matter under the New Covenant is so conspicuous that we should be very careful about putting something into His worship that He gives no indication of desiring. Presumption is to be avoided.

History. Historically, the evidence that early Christians used instruments in their worship is lacking. The documented use of instruments does not occur for centuries later, within a Roman Catholic context, and even many of the reformers, like John Calvin, were solidly against their use. For example, Calvin, in his commentary on Psalm 33, argued in the context of speaking about bringing in instruments, "To proceed beyond what we are there warranted by him [Paul] is not only, I must say, unadvised zeal, but wicked and perverse obstinacy." The use of instruments outside of the Roman Catholic context is, historically speaking, relatively new. The weight against the use of instrumental music in worship is historically strong and not to be lightly discarded.

Jewish Synagogue Model. It is sometimes argued that assemblies of Christians were modeled after the Jewish synagogues, yet Jewish worship in the synagogues did not entail the use of instruments, for the Jews saw instruments as connected to the temple. After the temple was destroyed, they refrained from recreating those instruments outside of that context. Even many modern synagogues still refrain from instrumental music (though they are divided on the issue). A simple search will show varying perspectives on this. Jewish Rabbi David Auerbach, who defends instruments if they enhance "the mitzvah of public worship," writes,

"There are those who claim that musical instruments should not be used in the synagogue service because it is an imitation of gentile (i.e. non-Jewish) practice. In its early years, the Church also prohibited instrumental music because it was considered secular and might lead to licentiousness. The Syrian, Jacobite and Nestorian churches still prohibit instrumental music." (http://www.jewishperspectives.com/music.asp)

Division. While everyone can agree that singing is desired by God under the New Covenant Scriptures, not everyone will agree on the use of instruments in public worship. Therefore, instrumental music is divisive in a congregational setting. Many, though not all, will concede that someone who wants to use instruments in their own private setting are free to do so as they live with their own consciences, but bringing it into the public setting will force it upon others and thus create a divisive situation. Others will respond that if the whole congregation agrees on their use, then no division has occurred and this objection is nullified. It is likely that this objection will not be quite as persuasive now as it might have been when instruments were initially being introduced and causing obvious splits. Yet, should unity not still be a consideration in what a group decides about a practice that will involve everyone?

Pushing a practice out of self-will should never be an option for a Christian, especially when admitting that such a practice is unnecessary, if not wrong.

Instruments Under the Old Law

Here we will elaborate on the point about instruments being part of the old Law. There is an interesting principle, used by Price, sometimes called The "Regulative Principle." This is stated in the Baptist Confession of Faith of 1689:

"But the acceptable way of worshipping the true God, is instituted by Himself, and so limited by His own revealed will, that He may not be worshipped according to the imaginations and devices of men, nor the suggestions of Satan, under any visible representations, or any other way not prescribed in the Holy Scriptures."

God's regulations of instruments in the Old Testament are in conjunction with tabernacle and temple worship. Instruments were under divine command and were not a matter of indifference or liberty for the Jews to whom the commands were given.

Price points out the following in conjunction with noting that the instruments were given in association with the temple:

1. The Old Testament temple worship in all of its outward ceremonies and rituals have been abolished.
2. For the worship of the church, we must look to Christ and His apostles to establish God's will for Christians on this matter.
3. "With no command, example, or any indication whatsoever" that the Lord desires instrumental music in public worship, we have no warrant for their use.

God was not silent about instruments in the Hebrew Scriptures, so their use was not presumptuous. There were specified "regulations of divine worship and the earthly sanctuary" (Heb. 9:1). The instruments were part of these regulations.

Moses was given specific instructions regarding the use of the trumpet, including even how it was to be made (Numbers 10). The trumpets would summon the people to the Tabernacle (vv. 1-3). If only one trumpet was used, then only the leaders would assemble (vs. 4). When used as an alarm, the various tribes around the tabernacle would move out (vv. 5-6). Only the priests, the sons of Aaron, were given the right to blow the trumpets (vs. 8). They would also be used to sound an alarm for battle (vs. 9), and for the appointed feasts (vs. 10). God regulated the instrument, how many were used, and the occasion for their use. That contrasts with pagan worship.

Instruments were commanded during the time of David in preparation for the temple, and God was particular about them — what they were, who would play them, when and where they would be played. In other words, their use of instruments was not a matter of self-appointed talent and desire that they expected God to rubber-stamp, but rather it was an issue of God's authority: "for the command was from the Lord through His prophets" (2 Chron 29:25). David appointed singers and musicians as directed by God in the details of the pattern given him (1 Chron. 16:1-6; 23:1-5; 28:19).

Why? Note, first, how detailed the pattern was for the temple in 1 Chronicles 28:11-13 and 19.

"Then David gave to his son Solomon the plan of the porch of the temple, its buildings, its storehouses, its upper rooms, its inner rooms and the room for the mercy seat; and the plan of all that he had in mind, for the courts of the house of the Lord, and for all the surrounding rooms, for the storehouses of the house of God and for the storehouses of the dedicated things; also for the divisions of the priests and the Levites and for all the work of the service of the house of the Lord and for all the utensils of service in the house of the Lord" (1 Chron. 28:11-13). "All this," said David, "the Lord made me understand in writing by His hand upon me, all the details of this pattern" (vs. 19).

Next, note the connection to the instruments in 2 Chronicles 29:25-28, during the days of Hezekiah's reformation efforts.

"He then stationed the Levites in the house of the Lord with cymbals, with harps and with lyres, according to the command of David and of Gad the king's seer, and of Nathan the prophet; for the command was from the Lord through His prophets. The Levites stood with the musical instruments of David, and the priests with the trumpets. Then Hezekiah gave the order to offer the burnt offering on the altar. When the burnt offering began, the song to the Lord also began with the trumpets, accompanied by the instruments of David, king of Israel. While the whole assembly worshiped, the singers also sang and the trumpets sounded; all this continued until the burnt offering was finished" (2 Chron. 29:25-28).

The "command of David" was the command of God. It wasn't an arbitrary decision made by David. If we follow the command through the Old Testament, we see that there is a consistent application:

1. Solomon (2 Chron. 5:11-13).
2. Jehoiada (2 Chron. 23:18).
3. Hezekiah (2 Chron. 29:25-28). Contextually, the playing of the instruments in Hezekiah's reforms worked in conjunction with the burnt offerings (see 2 Chron. 29-30 where all of this was re-established under Hezekiah as being what God wanted).
4. Josiah (2 Chron. 35:4, 15).

5. Return from captivity (Ezra 3:10).

6. Reforms of Nehemiah (Neh. 12:24, 35-36, 45-46).

7. The temple context of the psalms follows the pattern.

Here, then, is what we see in the Hebrew Scriptures: worship, including instrumental music (just as with sacrifices), was under God's divine authority. They practiced it in worship because God commanded it! Has God somehow relinquished His authority over worship now? If Old Testament temple worship, with its attendant practices, was abolished or intended to be a shadow pointing to a greater substance in Christ, then we must look to Christ and the apostles for what to do now.

The same Law system that had them offering the burnt offerings also had them playing the instruments at the temple. Let that sink in for a moment. This is the Law system that has been fulfilled in Christ. To take one part of that system as a justification for modern practice, but not take the other part, is to be guilty of proof-texting and misappropriating the passages to favor one's desired position.

What if we used the same arguments to justify modern day animal sacrifices or a separate priesthood? Why are we not hearing those arguments for these practices? They are part of the same system. If the arguments work for one, they work for the other. For example, would the following work?

Excursus: An Argument From Animal Sacrifices?

Please note that the point of the following is not actually to defend animal sacrifices, but simply to show that the same arguments made on behalf of instruments may be made on behalf of continuing animal sacrifices. Yet if we know that animal sacrifices have been fulfilled and are no longer what God wants, why wouldn't we understand the same for other "regulations of divine worship and the earthly sanctuary" (Heb. 9:1)?

1. People argue that God doesn't specifically condemn instruments in the New Testament Scriptures, but where does God condemn making all animal sacrifices in the same Scriptures? We can argue they are fulfilled, and this is true, but where are they condemned? We might argue against the sacrifices intended to cover sin (as in Hebrews), but that's not all of them. Will someone go to hell for offering animal sacrifices? Why should this be a matter of fellowship? Shouldn't there be a specific prohibition against all animal sacrifices in order to know they are wrong today? The point? One can make the same argument for animal sacrifices, so why aren't people defending them today?

2. Animal sacrifices were not just an aid to worship in the Old Testament. They were an integral part of worship (cf. 1 Chron. 16:29). In the New Testament, Christians are warned against eating things sacrificed to idols (Acts 15:29), but this is not against sacrificing in general. As long as we aren't sacrificing to idols or eating blood, what's the problem?

3. Animal sacrifices were performed and accepted prior to the giving of the Law. Since it was not something just for the Law, then it is meant for all time (so the argument would go). Didn't Paul go to the temple and participate in something to this effect?

4. People argue that instruments are found in heaven in the book of Revelation, and this proves that God wants it in the church now. However, the altar with its fire is also found in heaven in the book of Revelation (Rev 8). Does this show that God would approve of our offering up animal sacrifices today? Why would the altar for sacrifice be in heaven but not in the church? Perhaps an understanding of the nature of the book of Revelation would help resolve this.

5. People argue that instruments are found in the Psalms, and this

shows that God is pleased with them. However, animal sacrifices are also found in the psalms (for example, Psalm 51:19). David would offer up sacrifices that were pleasing to God. Would this prove that we should be offering these same sacrifices today?

6. People argue that since Jesus went to the temple, and the temple had instruments, then Jesus must have approved of them. However, Jesus must have participated and approved of animal sacrifices, too. He went to the temple and surely would have been accepting of them. He did, in fact, eat of the passover lamb. Yet all of this occurred under the Law and prior to His death and resurrection when He ushered in the New Covenant.

7. Some argue based on God's consistency. Since God wanted instruments under the Law, He wouldn't oppose them now. Yes, God is consistent, but would we also argue that since He commanded and wanted animal sacrifices in the Law, He wouldn't oppose them now?

Since the very same arguments for animal sacrifices may be advanced as for instrumental music in corporate worship, and since instrumental music is so widely accepted, practiced, and defended, whereas animal sacrifices by those claiming to follow Scripture are not widely accepted, practiced, and defended, we can only assume that the reason for this has to do with preferences and desires rather than a real sense of conviction that instruments ought to be used. If the arguments for the instruments are strong and move us in the direction of practice, why not the same for the animal sacrifices? If the argument is just that we have the liberty to do so, then this underscores the point that it has much more to do with personal desires than it does actual arguments from Scripture that convict us on the matter.

Is it not odd that those who would argue so strongly against a Law-keeping mentality (what they call "legalism") will argue for a practice that is grounded in the Law system, then call those who oppose it the "legalists"? How is not wanting to be presumptuous being legalistic? How is trying to use the Law as justification not a problem? If the argument for the practice is founded upon a Law system that they stringently believe is not a part of our system of grace, then why appeal to it as justification for modern practice under a New Covenant?

Aren't there principles that we carry across? Of course there are (cf. Rom 15:4, and see below). What has changed are not the principles or the character of God, but the stipulations, the "regulations of divine worship and the earthly sanctuary." The stipulations included the Laws, commandments, and expectations surrounding the priesthood, sacrifices, and and temple. Included in these commands, from the time of David, were God's instructions on the use of instruments for His worship.

If people wish to find justification for the use of musical instruments in corporate worship today, they won't find it based on appealing to the Law without also justifying continued ritual burnt offerings, circumcision (as a sign of the covenant), the Aaronic Priesthood, and the host of other Laws that went together. Those who would be offended at the suggestion that we bring back animal sacrifices based on the Law should also be offended at the suggestion that we bring back the instruments based on the Law. Why? Because they represent the same Law system we all agree cannot justify us, not the new covenant system of grace. If authority for the instruments is to be found, it will not be in the stipulations of the old Law. Justification for the practice needs to be found another way or abandoned. We must look to Christ.

Back to New Testament Principles

The Old Testament temple worship in all of its outward ceremonies and rituals have been fulfilled. For worship in the church, we must look to Christ and His apostles to establish God's will for Christians on this matter. As Price puts it, "With no command, example, or any indication whatsoever" that the Lord desires instrumental music in public worship under Christ, we have no warrant for their use.

This means that we must look to Christ and His apostles and prophets for authority. Since God is still in charge of His worship, we must ask: Has God authorized the use of musical instruments for worship in his church? Immediately, one might ask, "But doesn't the fact that it's in the Old Testament mean God would approve of it?" Again, does Old Testament practice based on the Law for Israel give authority for New Testament worship? Remember the animal sacrifices? If it authorizes one, why wouldn't it authorize the other? Now there is more we need to say about this.

Many practices from the Law of Moses were not meant to reach beyond the temple practices and worship (such as the sacrifices and levitical priesthood). We've already established that the command for instruments in the Law was connected to the levitical priesthood and temple worship. There is no temple ceremony to be brought forward since the levitical priesthood was abolished. Given that the ones who had the God-given authority (levitical priests) to engage the practices of the temple are no longer viable (no levitical priests exist today), then the practices associated with their position are also no longer viable. Who will play them by God's authority?

What does the New Testament say about justifying practices from the Law of Moses? Here is a sampling:

"For when the priesthood is changed, of necessity there takes place a change of law also. For the one concerning whom these things are spoken belongs to another tribe, from which no one has officiated at the altar. For it is evident that our Lord was descended from Judah, a tribe with reference to which Moses spoke nothing concerning priests." (Heb. 7:12-14)

"When He said, 'A new covenant,' He has made the first obsolete. But whatever is becoming obsolete and growing old is ready to disappear" (Heb. 8:13).

"The Holy Spirit is signifying this, that the way into the holy place has not yet been disclosed while the outer tabernacle is still standing, which is a symbol for the present time. Accordingly both gifts and sacrifices are offered which cannot make the worshiper perfect in conscience, since they relate only to food and drink and various washings, regulations for the body imposed until a time of reformation" (Heb. 9:8-10).

"For indeed what had glory, in this case has no glory because of the glory that surpasses it. For if that which fades away was with glory, much more that which remains is in glory" (2 Cor. 3:10-11).

"I testify again to every man who receives circumcision, that he is under obligation to keep the whole Law. You have been severed from Christ, you who are seeking to be justified by law; you have fallen from grace" (Gal. 5:3-4).

More passages may be cited, but these suffice to show that the practices associated with the Law of Moses are not the authority for what we do now. The point is that for the worship in the church, we must look to Christ and His apostles to establish God's will for Christians on this matter.

The question, then, is simply this: are mechanical musical instruments to be used in the church? If so, what instruments are to be used? Remember that under the Law God commanded the use and specified exactly the instruments, who played them, and on what occasions, and that is not the Law we are now under (Rom. 6:14). The New Testament answer to this question is silence. In other words, there are no mechanical instruments authorized in the New Testament. While *psallo-ing* is to be done with the heart (Eph. 5:19), this is not the same as using mechanical instruments.

Did God inadvertently leave out mechanical instruments, or did He intend to leave them out? Do we have the right to assume it given that 1) God is still in control of His worship, 2) God was so specific about them in the Law, and 3) we can find no indication that He wants them in the church now?

The differences between Old and New on this point are significant, and it is important to notice this contrast: in the Old, God was specific about both singing and playing. In the New, God is specific about singing, but not a word about playing anything mechanical in worship. In the Old, when temple worship was restored (as under Hezekiah), they looked to the "command of David" to make sure they were doing it as God designed it. In the New, there is no "command of David" appealed to; we can only look to Christ and His apostles.

The bottom line is that God has not left His worship open to our whims and desires. God regulates worship, including the use of instruments. If God left it out on purpose, who are we to put it back in?

An Argument from Fulfillment

There is another way of thinking about instruments that we might sometimes overlook. How should we view instruments now? Rather than just arguing that these have been "done away with," they can be thought of as being fulfilled in Christ, just as the sacrifices, priesthood, and other items under the Law. How are instruments of music Fulfilled in Christ?

Think about the patterns of Scripture. The more we study the

Scriptures as a whole, the more impressive is the idea of Christ fulfilling the Law. The concept runs deep and wide. Jesus said, "Do not think that I came to abolish the Law or the Prophets; I did not come to abolish but to fulfill" (Matt 5:17). We see this working in so many ways even in statements and events that are not necessarily "Law." For example:

1. He fulfills the image of God perfectly (Heb 1:3).
2. He fulfills the Exodus by providing the greatest exodus of all out of the slavery of sin (John 8:31ff).
3. He is the Prophet like Moses (Acts 3).
4. He is the Lawgiver (James 2).
5. He fulfills the Passover as the Lamb of God who takes away the sins of the world (1 Cor 5:7; John 1:29).
6. He fulfills the role of High Priest (Heb 5-8).
7. He fulfills the Davidic promise of the King who built the House of God in the greatest sense (Acts 2, 13, Matt 16:18).
8. He fulfills the tabernacle / temple as God dwelling among His people in the flesh (John 1:14).
9. He fulfills all the sacrifices (Heb 9-10).
10. He fulfills the seed promise to Abraham (Gal 3:16-17).

The list can go on, but it doesn't stop with Jesus. His body (His people, His church), also, fulfills specific aspects of what the Law represented. For example:

1. We are the completion of the nation promise (1 Pet 2:9).
2. We are the fulfillment of the levitical priesthood as a kingdom of priests (1 Pet 2:9; Rev 1).
3. We are, with Christ, the fulfillment of the temple (1 Cor 3).
4. We are, with Christ, the fulfillment of the sacrifices (Rom 12:1-2; Heb 13).
5. As the priests were to wear garments that represented holiness, so we put on Christ and are to live our lives adorned with holiness (Rom 13:14).

6. We are the fulfillment of the true circumcision, "who worship in the Spirit of God and glory in Christ Jesus and put no confidence in the flesh" (Phil 3:3).

7. We partake of the Lord's Supper as fulfillment of the Passover and feast of Unleavened Bread — feasts that showed the end of slavery and beginning of a new life because Christ our Passover has been sacrificed (1 Cor. 5:7).

We don't want to overdo it, but we can see that God intended for specific actions under the Old Covenant to represent spiritual qualities for fulfillment in the New Covenant. God didn't do anything without meaning, and it is this very point that we want to explore with reference to the instruments of music, by asking this next question:

How are instruments fulfilled in Christ?

The basic answer is that instruments are fulfilled in Christ through His people. Like other regulations of the Law and promises, instruments have a typological significance in terms of praise. Just as there was a special priesthood under the Law, there were also special singers and instrumental players under the Law.

Under Christ, all of God's people fulfill this purpose of praising God and proclaiming His excellencies (1 Pet. 2:9). Under Christ, all of us form a kingdom of priests and all share equally in the duties of praise.

God tells us to praise him through vocal singing, and the instruments to be played (as it were) are our hearts: "singing and making melody with your heart to the Lord" (Eph 5:19; Col 3:16). Here the instrument accompanying the singing is the heart. It is not enough simply to move lips, but the heart must also be moved. All of us are the priests, all of us are the singers, and all of us are the instruments of praise—and this would extend beyond the assemblies into one's life of holiness.

Bear in mind that what Ephesians 5:19 says applies to all Christians, not just a select group. Some argue that the passage includes the use of instruments (from the term *psallo*), but if God is telling one to play instruments, He is telling all to play. The truth is, he is telling all to "make melody in the heart." That is done independently of mechanical instruments, and it applies equally to every Christian. Everyone can sing. It's not about carrying a tune as much as expressing what ought to be in the heart — praise and thanksgiving for God and a desire to build up one another.

John Calvin wrote in his commentary on Psalm 33, that when they "frequent their sacred assemblies, musical instruments in celebrating the praises of God would be no more suitable than the burning of incense, the lighting up of lamps, and the restoration of the other shadows of the law." The argument here is against resurrecting the shadows of the Law, of which instruments were a part. With this we can agree.

We should clarify that our reason for refraining from an activity is not just because that activity is found under the Law. Those in Israel taught and sang, too. Yet God has told us how to praise Him through song as we *psallo* in our hearts to the Lord. The fulfillment of these activities is found in the way that we tune our hearts to His glory. "I will put My Laws in their hearts," God said through Jeremiah. This doesn't mean that He didn't want it in their hearts before, but it does show the emphasis that God intends. It is not through the outward ways by which He had Israel express themselves — a visible priesthood, animal sacrifices, instruments of music, specific clothing, etc. All of these are fulfilled in the hearts of God's people as they offer up themselves as living sacrifices. Our clothing is Christ. We are His instruments for praise. We are His priesthood. So why do we still sing and teach? Because that's what

God has expressed as His desire. The bottom line is still that it is an issue of God's desire, not ours. He has the right to tell us what praises Him.

Do we, then, believe in instruments of music today? In fulfillment, yes. We believe that we, His people, are the fulfillment of the shadow cast by the mechanical instruments under the old system. They were given for a reason in connection with the temple. They were part of the "regulations of divine worship and the earthly sanctuary" (Heb. 9:1). We, then, in connection with being God's temple now, are also the holy priesthood in holy array, offering ourselves as the spiritual sacrifices, presenting ourselves as the instruments for praise, and offering up prayers as incense. What began in the temple is fulfilled in us and will find its ultimate completion before God in heaven (see Revelation 15 where that imagery is carried forward).

When we focus on physical, mechanical instruments, we are missing the bigger picture. It wasn't the physical temple God was ultimately interested in. It wasn't the animal sacrifices, the incense, the levitical priesthood or the instruments He ultimately wanted. All these were shadows of the greater fulfillment found in Christ. Instead, let us focus on how we, as God's people, ought to be a holy temple, a royal priesthood, a holy nation, and instruments of praise for Him now. Don't focus on the shadow. Focus on the substance, for this is what God really wants. To further understand this, let's reflect on John 4.

In Spirit and Truth

"Jesus said to her, 'Woman, believe Me, an hour is coming when neither in this mountain nor in Jerusalem will you worship the Father. You worship what you do not know; we worship what we know, for salvation is from the Jews. But an hour is coming, and now is, when the true worshipers will worship the Father in spirit and truth; for such people the Father seeks to be His worshipers. God is spirit, and those who worship Him must worship in spirit and truth." (John 4:21-24)

How often do we look at this passage and think, "Well, God wants us to worship from the heart, and He wants us to worship according to truth"? This is true, of course, but are we missing some even greater concepts based in the context of John? Jesus was showing the woman that God had in mind something much greater than just worshipping at this place or that (like Jerusalem).

Jerusalem would have stood, not just for a city, but for everything unique to the worship engaged in by the Jews under the Law system. The temple, the sacrifices, the priesthood, the instruments, and other regulations of the divine sanctuary were all wrapped up in Jerusalem. To say that Jerusalem would not be the place "men ought to worship" is to say that all that Jerusalem stood for under the Law would no longer be what God was looking for under Christ. Something changed. No longer would His people worship according to the types and shadows of the Law, but in the spiritual reality that these represented (see Heb. 9-10). "In spirit and truth," then, is a much bigger concept that incorporates not just true worship from the heart, but moving beyond the types and shadows into the spiritual substance that these types represented.

Compare what Paul wrote to the Philippians: "for we are the true circumcision, who worship in the Spirit of God and glory in Christ Jesus and put no confidence in the flesh" (Phil. 3:3). Physical circumcision represented something much greater. It was a shadow. Those who worship in spirit and truth will move beyond the shadows into the substance that the shadows represented.

This is why we don't offer sin offerings and animal sacrifices, have a separate priesthood, a physical temple, musical instruments, the burning of the incenses, etc. All of these were part of the temple worship at Jerusalem. All of these were part of the "divine worship and the earthly sanctuary" (Heb. 9:1). Now we are to worship in the spiritual reality that these foreshadowed — in spirit and truth.

Origen (ca. AD 185-254) made a similar point in his commentary on this passage: "We too aspire to know how God is spirit as the Son reveals it, and to worship God in the spirit that gives life and not in the letter that kills. We want to honor God in truth and no longer in types, shadows and examples even as the angels do not serve God in examples and the shadow of heavenly realities but in realities that belong to the spiritual and heavenly order" (*Commentary on the Gospel of John, 13.145-146*).

Objections

"But God has given us talents and wants us to use those talents."

No one is saying not to use your talents to glorify God. The issue is not using talents. The issue is what God has expressed as His desire in our congregational worship for Him. If we follow the logic of this objection, then we must also say that we should have video gaming in worship, cooking in worship, sports in worship, construction in worship, etc. Are there any talents that would be out, or is anything and everything that is a legitimate talent to be part of congregational worship and public assembly? Use your talents for the glory of God, including your musical abilities, but when it comes to how God wants us to worship Him in this special sense when the church gathers, that is His call, not ours. What does He want?

"But the word for 'psalm' in Ephesians 5:19 and Colossians 3:16 means to pluck the strings of an instrument."

Actually, plucking the strings of a mechanical instrument is not inherent in the definition of *psallo* or *psalms*. The New Testament shows that the the *psalming* is to be done with the heart. Compare, for example, Psalm 33:2 in a temple context, "Sing praises to Him with a harp of ten strings," with Ephesians 5:19, "singing and making melody (*psallo*) with your heart to the Lord." The mechanical instruments were an application of the term from the Old Testament, but the term itself doesn't inherently entail mechanical instruments.

Further, the terms used in the text — psalms, hymns, and spiritual songs — are difficult to distinguish in any real, practical way. Notice, also, the context: "speaking … in psalms, hymns, and spiritual songs … making melody with the heart to the Lord." This is something that all Christians are responsible for, and it doesn't require mechanical instruments to do it.

If the mechanical instruments are inherently found in the definition, this would not explain why early Christians did not use the mechanical instruments that are alleged to be part of the definition. Definition is based on usage, and the usage of the term by the first century indicated a song of praise. Early Christians did not see the term as involving mechanical instruments.

Concerning the term *psallo*, think also about James 5:13, "Is anyone cheerful? He is to sing praises." In the Law, instruments were played in the context of the temple (as argued), with particular priests appointed to play specific instruments. The Jews would not have thought in terms of this being opened up to just anyone playing for worship based on talent. They didn't use instruments in the synagogues because, again, they saw them tied to the temple. Therefore, it is highly doubtful that James, writing to the dispersion (i.e., not in Jerusalem or near the temple), would have intended that they understand the term to include instruments. It just meant to sing praises, and that's the way translations recognize it. If *psallo*, in this case, meant to include instruments, then it would have been a departure for the Jews of the dispersion to start playing instruments in worship while they were away from the temple. Since *psallo* does not inherently carry with it the idea of instruments, there is no reason to think James meant for the Jews to think it should. The same would hold true for Paul's use of *psalmos* or *psallo* in Ephesians 5:19 and Colossians 3:16. These epistles were addressed to those who weren't even close to Jerusalem or the temple and there would have been no reason for them to think Paul meant to include mechanical instruments when that wasn't their practice apart from temple worship.

However, all of this still misses the point of the argument: we are the fulfillment of the instruments. The instruments, like the temple, the sacrifices, and the priesthood, were shadows. Ephesians 5:19 and Colossians 3:16 support the point being made here. The psalms are being sung with instruments of the heart, and we are the instruments.

"But what about the instruments in the book of Revelation?"

"Harps of God" are found in Revelation 15:2 (they are also used as simile in 14:2 where a voice was heard that sound like harpists playing on harps). In 15:2, the harps are being held by those who were victorious over the beast. Yet simply reading the context shows why this is not the passage authorizing mechanical instruments in church worship. In the same context we also find seven angels and seven plagues, a sea of glass, the beast and his image, the temple, and bowls of wrath among other items. Please read it. The language of Revelation is highly symbolic, not intended as a literal check list of items to use in worship. Further, if something being present in the book of Revelation is what authorizes it for congregational worship, we might also note, in the book, the golden altar, the burning of incense, the fire of the censers, reapers with sharp sickles coming out of the temple, and many more figures appropriate to such a work. There are far too many to list, but then that's the point. The book is replete with symbols. Shall we literalize all of these? Would this really be considered an appropriate way to interpret and apply the text of Revelation? Yes, these items stand for something (a study on its own), but we would need more information before we can use these texts to say that God wants mechanical instruments in congregational worship any more than he wants another physical temple built with an altar for burning incense.

"Where is your authority for singing harmony?"

Sometimes this question comes on the heels of the other objections failing. It's a move that attempts to say that since we do something unauthorized (singing in four-part harmony), then instruments must be okay, too. Of course, if singing in four-part harmony is unauthorized, then we need to quit doing it rather than using that as an excuse to do something else unauthorized.

What authorizes harmony is simply the fact that we are still singing. Something doesn't have to be specified when it fits under the general category that is permitted. All the text tells us is that we are to sing. It says nothing of style, tune, tempo, or pitch, yet all of these are necessary to some degree in order to sing anything (try singing without them). Since singing requires these, and since there is nothing else specified, then we must conclude that as long as we are singing, the style, tune, tempo, and pitch are authorized by the general command to sing. Singing harmony is simply a style, not a departure from singing. Other principles, such as our respect for God and others, orderliness, and need for edification, would also help guide what we sing and how we sing.

Conclusion

It is no small matter to strive to do things the way God has set them up. While we would love to be able to endorse mechanical instruments in the worship of the church if we had authority for them, we simply have no passage to which we can appeal that would support our case in the New Testament. While the examples in the Old Testament are very important, we understand that God set many practices up as types and shadows that would later be fulfilled in Christ and in His people. Instruments are one of those ordinances of the temple that now finds its fulfillment in the people of God.

The application of this should be seen: we are the temple. We are the priests. We are the sacrifices. We are the instruments of praise. May God help us be what He has called us to be!

Authority Options?

What are our options when it comes to authority? Consider the following four options, and ask, "Which of these is biblical defensible?"

1. We need God's authority for all that we do.
2. We need God's authority for most of what we do.
3. We need God's authority for some of what we do.
4. We need God's authority for none of what we do.

Which do you think is the viable option, and why? Let's think through them:

If options #2-4 are going to be defended, then they must be defended by an appeal to some kind of authority (self, another person or group, or God). But if #2-4 are approved by some authority that is not God, then what gives that approval any weight or power? "Because I say so"? Because another group says so? What gives them the authority? Do we have a right to say that our own authority is sufficient to carry the same weight as God's authority? If so, where do we get that idea? Then would we be able to boast about our own doing? If not, then the idea is a dead one, and we should give it up. If, however, #2-4 are approved by God in some way, then we are back to #1. Where in Scripture (or otherwise) is there any indication that God feels that anything less than #1 is acceptable? DM

Institutionalizing "Church"

Biblically, the church (*ekklesia*) is a group of people. Universally, the church is all of God's people everywhere (Heb. 12:23). The term also refers to a localized congregation (e.g., the church of God at Corinth, 1 Cor. 1:2), and can be narrowed down even more to when the group is actually assembled (1 Cor. 11:18; 14:23). Though the term "church" in English has been subjected to much abuse and thus has baggage, and though it was not the best term for translating *ekklesia*, we use the term here because it is what people are used to hearing when we speak of this subject. Because language is fluid, we can train ourselves to think "assembly," "congregation," or "group" when we hear the term, and thus use these terms interchangeably.

Let me say up front that I do not believe that every Christian is guilty of what I am about to address or that Christians want to purposefully avoid personal responsibility. I do not intend to overgeneralize or make accusations that indict well-meaning Christians who are striving to glorify God. I am trying to identify an attitude that I have seen and believe to be very dangerous, and it is possible that we aren't even aware of it. The problem can be quite subtle. I have been guilty of some of this thinking and have tried to identify areas with which we all might have some difficulty. I'll say more later, but none of this should be taken to belittle the group or group activity. The challenge is in trying to think properly about the individual's relationship to the group. Christ shed His blood and purchased the church, His assembly of people (Acts 20:28), so we surely would not want to minimize this great truth. The conclusions of this study are mine. If you believe they are flawed, or not clear enough, I am glad to discuss these matters further. All I can do is state and argue what I have concluded.

The problem addressed here is that of institutionalizing the "church." "Institutional" also has a few meanings, but what I'm talking about here is the idea of making something part of an established system, or restricting something to an establishment. When we do this, we think of the church as an entity all on its own, separated from all the individuals who comprise it. (Some may prefer putting all Christians in some other kind of institution, but that's not our subject now.)

Wikipedia (yes, actually) states the concept I'm wanting to convey: "The term 'institutionalization' is widely used in social theory to refer to the process of embedding something (for example a concept, a social role, a particular value or mode of behavior) within an organization, social system, or society as a whole." (http:// en.wikipedia.org/wiki/Institution#Institutionalization)

That definition describes how we might sometimes think of the church. We might embed our concepts and behavior into the system and lose sight of the individual. We are used to this kind of talk when it comes, say, to the Roman Catholic Church, where the "Church" is spoken of as an establishment separate from the people. But that problem is not just "theirs." Consider how this may happen among God's people today:

Christianity gets confined to the established institution. By this, I mean that we may be very concerned about what the church does as an institution, but we may not take as much care with our own personal lives. The church must be kept pure, we reason, and that means that the group must keep free from error. "It" must worship correctly, get a steady diet of right doctrine, and do the right works in the right way. Meanwhile, individually, our lives may be filled with impurity, greed, lust, malice, and other evils. By institutionalizing our concept of the church, we may end up engaging in mere ritualism rather than pure worship. The "church" is doing things right, we think, and as long as we "attend church," we must be okay.

Further, when the institution does something, then we may feel that we have done it because we are part of that institution (unless what they've done is bad, of course). Even though we might not have done anything but give a few dollars (if even that), we still count ourselves as having done whatever the institution has done as a whole. While there is some truth to the idea that our support (financial and otherwise) of something does involve us in the effort to some degree, institutionalized programs tend to salve our consciences even though we have done little. For example, if we have a program for evangelism, then we may feel that we are being evangelistic, even if we aren't personally trying to teach others. The "group" is doing it, and we are in the group, so we are doing it, we reason. Being listed in the directory of the group, however, is not a substitute for actually participating in what the group does.

Work and Worship gets confined to the institution. Here, we might tend to become the audience rather than the participants. I don't just mean in the worship activities when the group is assembled. We might watch others do the work. We may expect the preacher or the elders to take care of church business so we can have our nice little social club to attend. This, then, facilitates the idea that we become mere observers in worship, listening to and watching others, instead of being active participants. We "attend worship," but we may not actually engage in worship. We "enjoy worship" because we like what we hear and we feel lifted up, but we might not have actually praised God ourselves or helped much in lifting up others. When we institutionalize worship in the group, we make it more about what we get out of it as an audience rather than what we are giving to God as participants.

Identity becomes based on the group, rather than upon Christ. Our Christianity might come to be based more on how we identify the group rather than allegiance to Christ. For example, we might say, "I'm Church of Christ" instead of, "I'm a Christian." We think of "Church of Christ Preachers" rather than gospel preachers. This type of lingo betrays the institutionalized concept. As long as we are listed in the directory, part of that group, then we are okay. Institutionalization is at the heart of denominational and sectarian thinking. If we identify with the right name and the correct group, then all is well, right? Again, this concept pays little attention to personal holiness.

Doctrine gets institutionalized. We might ask, "What is the doctrine of the Church of Christ?" Questions like this betray the concept. Instead, we need to be asking, "What do the Scriptures teach?" "What does the Lord say?" We identify the group by particular doctrines, and this lends itself to "Group-think." If the church holds the right position on a doctrinal matter, then that's what really counts. We ask, "What do we believe about this or that?" It may not matter how much we know or what we believe as individuals. The answer is embedded in the institution, and we'll just go to the preacher or elders, or even a "brotherhood magazine" or something else, to learn what we are supposed to think. What matters is that the doctrine of the church is sound, and that soundness might be judged by some other source than Scripture, such as unwritten tradition (what "we've" always done). Personal belief and study can easily get shoved aside. What the "group" thinks is what counts.

Universal and Local Institutionalization. Again, Scripture speaks of the church in both universal and local terms. That God wants Christians to act together in certain ways is evident from Scripture, but both universal and local senses can also be thought of in this institutionalized sense. We need to be careful how we speak of all this. Christians universally do not act in some united way that abrogates any personal responsibilities. The universal assembly of God's people acts only in the sense of individual Christians acting. There is no universal organization or earthly headquarters. Even though the local group does have organization to it (elders, deacons, etc.), the group acting does not mean that any given individual is acting. Once again, institutionalization makes it so that, in our minds, we won't have as much personal obligation as long as the group is correct.

Salvation is Institutionalized. I'd be hard pressed to come up with a better example for this point than Robert Turner's Little Red Wagon illustration:

"It seems many think of the church as something like a little red wagon. 'Established on Pentecost' -- it stood ready to roll, and people could jump in and ride to heaven. But somewhere along the line a side-rail broke, an axle was bent, the tongue came loose, and finally a wheel fell away. Luther tried to put the wheel back on, but further bent the axle in his effort. Others replaced the tongue with a new but different instrument -- unsuited to the purpose and function of the original tongue. Alas, the church was broken down and out of service.

Then A. Campbell and Barton Stone determined to restore the church. They straightened the axle, replaced the tongue with an original model, repaired the side-rail and put the wheel back in place. Now people could again ride home to heaven." (*What Did God "Establish"?* Plain Talk, January 1964).

When we stand before God on the day of judgment, it will not be as a group, but as individuals (2 Cor. 5:10). We cannot afford to think that as long as I'm in the right group (the wagon), I'll be fine. We might just be in the "right group," yet personally be lost because we have neglected our salvation.

Institutionalization Twice Removed. What I mean here is the problem of one "institution" (the "church") becoming a collection agency for other, separate institutions. Over the years, congregations have split over the question of whether the church can donate to human institutions (orphan homes, colleges, etc.). I won't go into the whole matter here, but one of the problems I have with this practice is that it doubles down on the concept, starting with that initial institutionalization of the church. This complicates matters because we may already be under the impression that we can transfer personal responsibility to the group. Then the group transfers those responsibilities to other institutions and we keep pushing personal duty down the road. We can make an argument about whether or not such congregational action is authorized in the first place, but what we ought to see is that the more institutionally-minded we become, the further we get from personal responsibility. We are kicking the can down the road for someone else to pick up. I believe that a fundamental flaw of this form of institutionalism is that we have already institutionalized the "church" in our minds, creating a faulty view of what the church really is and how "it" works.

No institution can substitute for personal responsibilities. Take James 1:26-27 as an example: "If anyone thinks himself to be religious, and yet does not bridle his tongue but deceives his own heart, this man's religion is worthless. Pure and undefiled religion in the sight of our God and Father is this: to visit orphans and widows in their distress, and to keep oneself unstained by the world."

That this passage teaches personal obligation is clear. The institutionalization of this concept would mean that we pass this off onto the church instead of personally seeking to fulfill these things. Instead of my doing it, the "church" does it. Scripture elsewhere tells us that, unless there is a true widow (I.e., truly destitute), "let not the church be burdened" (1 Tim. 5:16). The group doesn't come into play until individuals fulfill their own responsibilities, but we might be seeking to have the group do it for us. Then, to make it twice removed, we may think that if we donate some money to the church, then the church donates money to another institution that then oversees the work, we have really fulfilled James 1. We haven't. Whatever the group does is not in itself a substitute for personal duty, whether once or twice removed.

This point should not be construed to mean that an individual can never use the services of an institution. I can take a family member to a hospital and still maintain my oversight of responsibility while using the services of the institution (as opposed to just dropping someone off at the hospital and thinking, "it's all on them now. Let them deal with it."). The problem of institutionalized thinking, as I'm addressing it, is thinking that by using an institution (like the church, if we think of the church that way) we have fulfilled all we need to do. As an individual, if I am going to use the services of an institution, particularly for something important, I would still want to maintain oversight and be very much involved in what is going on. For example, parents who send their children to schools can maintain careful oversight of their children's education rather than thinking they need do nothing else but drop their children off at school and let the school handle it all. People who feel a keen sense of responsibility will be directly involved in what's going on, regardless of whose services they use in the process.

"Church" work necessitates individuals working. There is no "church machine" separate from the people to do the work. The only way the church can work is when individuals work. Ephesians 4:11-16 needs to be well engrained in our thinking. Each part doing its share causes the growth of the body. Think about it. We might say, "The work of the church is to teach the gospel." If we institutionalize this, then we push it off onto the group to have a program of some kind. If we think about it biblically, however, we will realize that the way the church teaches the gospel is through Christians teaching the gospel as they can, where they can, and to whom they can. The group can help facilitate this through its encouragement and resources, perhaps even with some type of "program," but the group cannot do anything unless individuals are doing something. Evangelism isn't really about establishing programs; it's about Christians proclaiming the excellencies of Him who called us out of darkness into His marvelous light (1 Pet. 2:9) whenever and wherever possible.

None of this should be taken to mean that the local group is of little importance, nor does it mean that "the church can do whatever the individual can do" (I'm sorry, but kissing one's spouse is not a church activity). Remember, Paul argued that individuals are responsible in certain matters where the group is not to be burdened (1 Tim. 5). Yet none of this means that we should shun all group action and just try to go it alone. God wants us to engage in certain activities with other Christians. He wants us meeting together so that we can encourage one another to love and good works (Heb. 10:23-25). What we do as a local group is important, and we still need to act according to the authority of God. For example, the Lord's Supper is put into an assembly context. Just because we individually eat a variety of foods at home does not mean that we can treat the Lord's Supper as if it were a common meal where we can substitute whatever we wish for the bread and fruit of the vine. Yet, even within that group action, the individual carries personal responsibility to examine self (1 Cor. 11:28). It is not the group's job to examine me in this matter.

The point is that we should not institutionalize the church in our minds and turn it into something that Scripture knows nothing about. The church is not a "thing" that exists apart from the Christians who comprise it. Let's all be the responsible Christians God has called us to be, for after all is said and done, all we can say is, "We are unworthy servants; we have only done what was our duty" (Luke 17:10, ESV).

The Individual and Church

We speak now of the individual and the organized local congregation. The twin fallacies of composition and division assume that what is true of the parts is true of the whole (composition), and what is true of the whole is true of the individual parts (division). Composition would take the basic form, "Individual pieces of x have characteristics Y and Z; therefore all of X has characteristics Y and Z." This is not always fallacious, but it cannot be assumed to be true without proper warrant. For example, one might reason that since particular players are the best at their position, then putting all the players together necessarily makes the best team (though they might not play so well as a team). Division would reverse composition. For example, since this is the best team in the league, then all the individual players are the best players at their position. (These are common illustrations.)

These fallacies can be instructive when thinking about the relationship of the individual to the congregation. It would be fallacious, for example, to say that what is true of the individual Christian is true of the congregation of which he is a part. Likewise, it is fallacious to say that whatever is true of the congregation as a whole is true of each individual Christian who is part of the group.

Once again we should be able to see how these fallacies might be committed. For example:

"These Christians are hypocrites; therefore the whole church is hypocritical."

"The church is evangelistic; therefore each Christian is evangelistic."

Both of these statements are fallacious. Hypocrites within a congregation do not make the entire group hypocritical, and a congregation that is overall actively evangelistic does not mean each individual is actively participating very well.

It is not uncommon to hear the argument, "Because the church is made up of individuals, then whatever the individual can do (or is doing), the church can do (or is doing)." This is the fallacy of composition. We can understand how the fallacy is made. The church is comprised of Christians, but individual Christians acting is not identical to the organized group as a whole acting. This is seen in passages like 1 Timothy 5, where believers are told to care for their own needy first (widows) so that the church is not burdened: "If any woman who is a believer has dependent widows, she must assist them and the church must not be burdened, so that it may assist those who are widows indeed" (vs. 16). This would make no sense at all if there is no distinction to be made between individual action and organized group action. Individuals act in their capacity as business associates, husbands, wives, mothers, fathers, citizens, neighbors, etc. These actions are independent of the organized group. No one would reasonably argue that since a husband and wife, both of whom are Christians, share an intimate relationship, this means the entire church shares that same relationship. Clearly, individuals can act on their own without their actions being that of the group. In matters of money, Peter told Ananias, who had just lied, that his land and money were under his (Ananias') control. We can understand that an individual maintains control of his own possessions and finances until relinquished to the group.

The church (group) is not an institution separate from people (as we have previously argued), but the group still does exist with organization and authorized actions; in this sense the church is an organization (i.e., a group of people organized for a particular goal or work). This organization need not be complicated, and we aren't using the term here to imply some massive business model.

Organization means that there is order to what is going on, under leadership, and has a goal and purpose to which all are attending. Is there biblical evidence for this?

1. The evidence for local congregations is found throughout the New Testament documents, particularly from Acts on. When congregations are addressed, these epistles take on more than simply the idea of Christians who all happen to live in the same city. The epistles were intended to be read in assemblies, implying that they met in order to hear God's word read and taught. The church at Corinth, for example, came together as a group (or were supposed to) with the intention of edifying, teaching, and participation in the Lord's Supper (1 Cor. 11:18ff; 14) . Instead of chaos, and since God is not the God of confusion (14:33), order and organization within the assembly itself was required.

2. The evidence for elders and deacons shows God's desire for local organization (Acts 20; Phil. 1:1; 1 Tim. 3; Titus 1). If we are to put ourselves under the "leaders" (Heb. 13:17), who keep watch for our souls, this cannot be done without some level of organization. They cannot do this if they do not know who it is that they are supposed to be watching for. This implies some kind of record, knowledge, roll, or something of which they would be aware. People often shy away from "membership" terms, but the idea is simply that the Christians know who is part of their group so they can help encourage and share their activities.

3. The evidence for organized, congregational action is strong. The very fact of assembling together for edification, hearing God's word, participating in the Lord's Supper, etc., is evidence of specified group action. Paul wrote of the "churches of Macedonia" acting by collecting funds to send back to needy saints in Jerusalem (2 Cor. 8:1ff; note that the plural form of ekklesia here implies local groups acting; if all Paul was doing was talking about Christians generally in the area, why would he use the plural form?). He directed the

"churches of Galatia," and then the church at Corinth, to collect funds for needy saints (1 Cor. 16:1-4). Any actions like these require some organization.

Authorization for individual action is not identical to authorization for congregational action. If the church is not to be burdened with some matters that the individual has an obligation toward, then this is proof enough of the point. The congregation exists for a purpose, and God has provided for particular activities within a congregational setting—Christians coming together for His purposes, and in which all are expected to participate in organized action.

The point is that we should not conflate individual action and authority with congregational action and authority. We understand this principle in other matters. If we gave funds to a hospital with an expectation that these funds are used for helping the sick, and they take these funds and form a softball team with it, we would likely be fairly upset with such a misuse. Does this mean we wouldn't support a softball team in another context? Of course not. This is simply recognizing the context and purpose for which a particular group or organization exists.

God wants Christians banding together in a congregational setting to worship Him and encourage one another in the things of Christ. We don't find congregations in Scripture acting in any and every way that individuals might act separately, though they are sometimes chastised for the way certain individuals act (e.g, 1 Corinthians; Revelation 2-3). "When you come together as a church" is instructive (1 Cor. 11:18), and they were limited by God's orders as to what they were to do in such a setting (1 Cor. 14:37). If no distinction is to be made between church and individual settings, then there would be no context in which the women could speak up (vs. 34).

Everyone participates in various organizations and relationships with different contexts and purposes. Christians might join together to form a business in one context (e.g., a donut shop), but this does not mean the "church" as a whole (congregational or universal) is in the donut business (composition fallacy). Christians working in conjunction with each other in education generally does not put the church in the education business. Context and purpose are everything (as in biblical interpretation, so in life application). In the capacity of a local congregation, there is a context and purpose that differs from other actions that may involve multiple Christians. Again, we recognize this principle in other areas of life. Players on the Giants team going to the movies together does not mean the "Giants" are going to the movies (this would imply a more official, organized context and purpose). There is a reason people speak about government abuses, where they recognize that there are limits to what a government ought to be able to do in relation to the individuals of the state. Again, organizations exist for different purposes and in different contexts. Why would this be any different when it comes to local congregations that exist on God's authority?

Though the congregation is comprised of individuals, the congregation as an organized group is not identical to the individual (division) and the individual is not identical to the congregation (composition). We do well to remember this in discussions about both individual and congregational activities.

The Simplicity is in the Details

Sometimes it is pointed out that there are few details about worship in the New Testament. This observation supposedly supports the notion that we don't really have much of a pattern for worship in the New Testament. This is set over against the Old Testament system, where so many details are spelled out.

Does this mean that there are no details in the New Testament? Does it mean that the details we have are unimportant?

Here is what I believe is overlooked in this: If we have so few details, then this must mean that the information we do have is very important. Why would we complicate things by adding to it?

The simplicity of worship under the New Covenant is found in those few details. There is nothing complicated about it, and it need not be embellished just because we want to add more to it. After all, if the stress is that the new covenant is not like the old, then why try to bring in details of the old covenant worship that the new covenant details leave out? Why complicate the simple? Why not be content with it as is? Or do we really think worship is more about what we want and like?

If it's revealed, then it must be pretty important, and we should pay attention. If it isn't revealed, then that, too, must be a pretty important part of what God intended to convey to us.

In other words, if the New Testament Scriptures keep it simple, so should we. DM

On the Church Support of Human Institutions

Part 1

Those who are familiar with the history of the Restoration Movement (as it is known) should also be familiar with the various divisions that have occurred among those who have attended churches of Christ. Among those divisions include the issue of whether or not a local church can or should donate funds to a human institution (or para-church organizations working independently of churches) such as a college, a missionary society, or an orphan's home. Sadly, some of these divisions fostered such strong feelings among so many that the damage of division, in large part, seems irreparable. I don't imagine that I will be able to bring together all the various factions that exist or repair the rifts that are now present. Many of these battles were fought by previous generations. By the time I was born, the divisions were already set, for the most part, and the damage was done. Churches were ripped apart and both brethren and families were split and torn. Certainly, if we could go back in time and change how that all turned out, we would. We cannot. Nevertheless, we can seek to understand positions and try to identify the critical elements that will help us move forward in a way that honors God, His work, and His way.

From what I can tell, there are, at least, three crucial components to the issue that helped foster the strong feelings. None of these are mutually exclusive, of course, but the emphases on these, without due balance and respect, might cause us to overlook one of the critical elements. These are: 1. Compassion and Love; 2. Conviction and Biblical Authority; and 3. Getting the Work Done.

All three of these components must be present if a local church is going to accomplish God's work in God's way. Succinctly, we might say it this way: With compassion and love, together with a proper respect for biblical authority, God desires for a local church to diligently work to evangelize, edify, worship, and provide for needy saints.

1. Compassion and Love.

That God desires for us to have compassion and show love is one of the most fundamental teachings of the Scriptures. The Lord desires compassion (Matt. 9:13), which reflects the fact that He shows compassion (Matt. 9:36). Christians are to "Put on a heart of compassion" (Col. 3:12) and show the kind of love that God has showed us: "Owe nothing to anyone except to love one another" because love fulfills the law (Rom. 13:8-10). Applying this kind of attitude toward the local church's work, then, is vital. We should have compassion on the lost, showing them the love of Christ by teaching them the gospel and seeking to save their souls. We should show love and compassion toward one another through the process of building each other up and finding proper ways to help each other in times of need, physically, spiritually, and financially.

2. Conviction and Biblical Authority.

Compassion and love do not override the need to be biblical. Both truth and love are vital (Eph. 4:15). We must seek to do God's work in God's way. Honoring God properly and doing all to His glory and in the name of the Lord necessarily entails respecting His word and working within the boundaries that He has given (Matt 7:21-23; Col. 3:17; 1 Pet. 4:11; Prov. 30:5-6, etc.). Therefore, conviction about how to do the work is important because it will directly reflect how dedicated we are to the authority of God and His revealed word. This can be done, while at the same time showing love and compassion. Since God is the One who defines love, then we must respect His revelation about how we should be showing that love, first for Him, and second for others. In short, what we find in Scripture regarding the local church getting the work done is this:

First, a local church has fellowship with preachers and in evangelism by giving direct support (Phil. 4:15; 2 Cor. 11:8). Never do we find another organization stepping between the congregation with her elders and the evangelist being supported.

Second, a local church provides for her own edification by the diligent teaching of those who serve in that position (Eph. 4:11-16). All members are taught to serve, and are encouraged to be part of the group doing their share.

Third, a local church provides benevolent aid to needy saints by directly making provisions for the needs. A local group may care for its own as necessary, but when benevolent needs are greater than one local group can bear, we find disciples sending funds for relief to the elders of the group in need (Acts 11:29-30). Once again, we never find another human institution standing between the local church and the work being supported.

All of these matters are cared for by the local churches and the elders shepherding the flock among them (1 Pet. 5:2). That is the pattern we find consistently when a local church is active. The pattern is uncomplicated and direct.

In part 2, for those who are interested in further explanation, we address the issue, in more detail, of whether or not churches should support human institutions.

3. Getting the Work Done.

Arguments over how to get the work done can overshadow the actual work, if we are not careful. Christians and churches need to be diligent in actually applying the biblical standards and getting the work accomplished. How it is done, as important as it is, won't matter if nothing is being done at all. Each local congregation needs to be dedicated to the teaching, preaching, building up her members, and identifying benevolent needs as they arise. A group needs to keep her eyes open to the opportunities, seeking the lost, reading and studying Scripture diligently, and willing to roll up her sleeves and actually do the work. This takes dedicated members who are willing to do their share (Eph. 4:16). A local group ought to be dedicated to honoring and glorifying God, respecting His authority, excelling in His work, and showing love for one another.

God's people seek for the unity of the Spirit in the bond of peace (Eph. 4:1-6). May God help us as we, individually, strive to glorify God, and as each local church seeks to honor God as the Scriptures show.

Part 2

Part 1 may be enough for some, but since the nature of the discussion is rarely so simple, here, I wish to outline some of my reasons for opposing a congregation's donating support to human institutions and businesses. The point is not to further divisions, but to seek unity based upon biblical precedent, and to seek a better understanding of the biblical idea of the local church and her work.

I can only speak for myself, not for a brotherhood at large. We make a mistake if we try to force a collective mentality by which we have some tangible way of measuring who is in or out of the "brotherhood." One of the dangerous side effects, if we are not careful, is the outgrowth of a denominational mindset whereby we try to centralize doctrines and enforce fellowship on a scale larger than the local church. Whereas biblically, the universal church has no organization and transcends time and space (Heb. 12:23), we tend to speak of the universal body as a more concrete object by calling "it" institutional or non-institutional. While there are local churches that support human institutions (often called "institutional") and those that do not support human institutions (often called "non-institutional"), the universal church is not "institutional" or "non-institutional." The local level is where the issue must be handled. One may argue that all of this is just a mode of expression to help us know where people stand, but I'm afraid it has the effect of muddying our concepts of the church. The "Church of Christ" is not a web composed of interconnected congregations on some universal level that centralizes its doctrines and practices.

Second, the labels typically will not help us achieve unity. Labels sometimes become short-cuts for pigeonholing people into their little boxes, but this may be done without true understanding of what these labels mean or convey. Further, they often widen the gap of division and serve to polarize brethren. If someone can just label me as an "anti," then the work is done and the well is poisoned. They need not deal with the issue or the positions involved (even though everyone is "anti" something). "Anti" says it all. A young man told me once that he had heard that all of us "antis" are just devils who would never lift a finger to help an orphan or care for a widow. Once he spent time with our group, he knew how false that impression was. The issue is not whether we should want to help people. The issue is whether or not there are any scriptural boundaries around how activities should be handled. On the other side, we may just call someone "liberal," which is vague and confusing at best. Yet again, it has the effect of shutting down the conversation if we aren't careful. Pejorative labels are lazy and they do not accomplish much positive.

With all of that said, now, I want to give some reasons why I oppose a congregation's donations that support human institutions. For clarity, I will include in this not only what the issue is, but what it is not.

1. The issue is not whether any institution whatsoever is permissible. I am not opposed to institutions altogether. For over 13 years I taught the Bible at a college. Is that inconsistent? I don't believe so, as long as the college stayed out of the treasuries of local churches. I believe there is a line there that ought not to be crossed. I have no problem with the existence of an orphan's home or a widow's home. The right for a business to exist and operate is not the issue; the issue is whether or not a congregation should be a donation conduit for the business or institution.

2. The issue is not whether or not a church can ever use the services of another business. There is a critical distinction to be made between using and paying for the services of a business and donating funds to the business. If a church makes a flyer and uses the services of a local printing business, then the group ought to pay for the services. That is very different from the church taking from its treasury to make a donation to that business, wherein no particular service was purchased and that business now uses those funds at their own discretion. A church may buy radio time for the purpose of spreading the gospel, but that is different from making a donation to a radio station.

Let's take this a step further. May a congregation take care of "widows indeed"? Yes, and 1 Timothy 5 is clear about that. The passage says, "If any woman who is a believer has dependent widows, she must assist them and the church must not be burdened, so that it may assist those who are widows indeed" (vs. 16). Paul draws a line between what the church should or should not "be burdened" with. Individuals need to care for their own so that the local congregation is not burdened with the care of those for whom individuals are responsible. Once that avenue has taken its course, the church may care for the true widow. How? There is some leeway to the how since it is not spelled out. We trust the elders and leaders of a group to make appropriate, biblically authorized decisions. May the church put the widow in a home and take care of her needs there? Yes, but that is not the same as making donations. That is taking responsibility and oversight for the situation at hand. The church would pay for the services, of course (there are no free tickets), but the church is still overseeing the care of that widow. It is personal and responsible. When the seven of Acts 6 took care of tables, there is no indication that they donated funds to some "serving tables" institution that then decided how to carry it out.

While I am not saying that people are wanting to be lazy (no intent to judge motives), there may be unintended consequences when a church simply makes donations to the organization rather than maintaining the oversight. The donation allows the business to make the decisions and do the work. The funds are spent on whatever that business decides. That business might even take care of widows who are not "widows indeed" (as Paul describes), thus involving the church, through her donations, in what Paul explicitly said should not happen. There is a difference between overseeing the work, which entails buying the necessary resources and paying for services on the one hand, and on the other hand collecting money to donate to an institution that will in turn make the decisions about who they are helping and where they will spend the money.

While it is true that giving money to a cause involves us in that cause (even if remotely), we cannot afford to think that giving money is the answer that relieves us from taking an active part of a work for which we are given personal responsibility. When an individual cares for her own elderly mother, she may use and pay for the services of a nursing home while still maintaining oversight. The individual will not likely think that just making a donation to the nursing home alleviates the personal responsibility of caring for her mother. When parents raise their children, they don't get off the hook by donating money to a child-rearing institution that then makes their decisions for them.

The way that we find the work being done in Scripture is that the local church, with the oversight of elders, takes care of her own work. The oversight of elders in a local group is limited to "the flock of God among" them (1 Pet. 5:2) and they do not have authority to extend that oversight to another flock. When a local church sends funds to an individual preacher, for example, they are having direct fellowship with the one who receives their funds. Biblical fellowship is personal; it does not pass through a secondary business, corporation, or human institution. Local churches are right to by-pass the human institutions and deal directly with the need. Elders may scripturally make decisions about congregational funds by sending funds to a preacher with whom they desire fellowship, and they may receive funds from elsewhere for benevolent help within that group (Acts 11:29-30), but in no cases do we find a congregation going through another human institution that, in turn, does the work of choosing who and what the money goes toward.

3. The issue is not whether an individual can support a business or institution. Families and individuals can do many things that would be inappropriate for the local church to do. Even the business world understands that there is a difference between personal business and corporate business, and many have gotten themselves into deep trouble by mixing the two (e.g., using the corporation for personal business is considered unethical). While the church is not a business per se, the congregation is a corporate body that exists for particular reasons.

Scripture teaches that there is a difference between the funds possessed by an individual and the funds that are part of a collective. Acts 5 illustrates this point. Ananias lied about what he did with his money, and Peter pointed out to him regarding the funds received from the sale of personal property, "While it remained unsold, did it not remain your own? And after it was sold, was it not under your control?" (vs. 4) Ananias had control and rights over the use of his own funds. So do we today. Yet, once funds are relinquished to the group, we also relinquish personal rights to those funds. They now belong to the group and ought to be used for proper and authorized purposes.

1 Timothy 5, again, tells us that there are boundaries that exist around what the local church ought to be "burdened" with. "The church must not be burdened" (vs. 16) is not something to slough off or treat lightly, and it is not just splitting hairs to insist on a distinction the apostle clearly makes.

4. The issue is whether or not we have biblical precedent for using the local church as a conduit for collecting funds for other businesses and institutions. The issue is one of authority. Is the local group authorized to use its funds in that kind of way in the first place? What passage would show this? One of the issues of the past was whether or not a church could donate to a "missionary society," so let's use this as a case in point. There is notable difference between donating to a missionary society and directly sending funds to a preacher of the gospel. One has biblical precedent; the other does not and is without biblical authority.

No one should have any problem recognizing that a church may send financial aid to a preacher, and thereby have fellowship with that preacher in the spread of the gospel (Phil. 4:15-16; 1 Cor. 9:8-14; 2 Cor. 11:8). Notice that the giving of the funds is itself joining in fellowship with the one who receives the funds. The fellowship is personal and direct between the local group and the preacher. The authority for this practice is clear and unequivocal. A missionary society, on the other hand, is a separate business that handles the work once the money is received by those in charge. When a church sends funds to the institution, the board of the organization makes decisions about where and how those funds are used. It is no longer in the hands of the local church or its elders. Further, the fellowship would be with the institution since it is the institution that receives and distributes the funds as it deems appropriate. The question is, do we find any indication in Scripture that would lead us to think that this latter way is how God desires for a local church to operate? Where is the passage or principle? Is congregational fellowship to be with individuals or with other human organizations?

5. What, then, is the solution to doing the needed work? There is likely frustration over the disagreements about method and authority, attended by a feeling that nothing actually gets done. Here, then, are some thoughts about that:

First, Local churches need to be committed to remaining autonomous and independent, as Scripture shows. Not only would this help them remain true to God's authority, but it would allow them to focus on the work themselves. Elders can focus on shepherding. The group can take personal responsibility in evangelism and in benevolent care when needed.

Second, individuals need to be committed to taking care of personal responsibilities. Scripture places a premium on personal obligation, just as Paul again pointed out in 1 Timothy 5. Further, James wrote, "If anyone thinks himself to be religious, and yet does not bridle his tongue but deceives his own heart, this man's religion is worthless. Pure and undefiled religion in the sight of our God and Father is this: to visit orphans and widows in their distress, and to keep oneself unstained by the world" (1:26-27).

While people have tried to make the case that this passage in James authorizes church supported donations to orphan's and widow's homes (distinct organizations separate from the local church), let's just read the text -- several times -- and see if it speaks to anything other than personal responsibility. The point here is not to discuss all the ins and outs of James 1, but to observe that personal responsibility is what's at issue, for this is the way that any person can "keep oneself unstained by the world." The congregation cannot do that for us. Another institution cannot do that for us. Another institution acting as a result of church donations cannot do that for us. Do we sometimes fail in our personal obligations? Yes, we do. But do we help ourselves by thinking that other institutions are taking care of things, thereby giving us a feeling of relief in the matter?

Conclusion

I have tried to outline a few of the problems associated with a congregation's donation support to other institutions and businesses while maintaining that local churches and individuals can accomplish the work intended by God. This can only practically be worked out on the local level. Both churches and individuals need to be committed to honoring God His way. By doing this, we can seek unity and be more effective in reaching out to a lost world, building each other up, and helping each other through difficult times. May God help us do so.

Led by the Spirit?

Being led by the Spirit is not about how we feel about something. If we are led by the Spirit, our feelings need to be brought under His subjection. To that end, the Spirit has given us an objective standard by which we can know that we are following His lead. The context of Romans 8 is a contrast between walking by the flesh and walking by the Spirit. If we are truly being led by the Spirit, we will set our minds on the things of the Spirit, "for if you are living according to the flesh, you must die; but if by the Spirit you are putting to death the deeds of the body, you will live" (Rom. 8:13). The "mind set on the Spirit" (vs. 6) will never ignore what the Spirit has revealed, for that is the only way we will know the mind of God (cf. 1 Cor. 2:10-13). The ones being led by the Spirit are the ones paying attention to His revelation. Feelings will follow, not lead. Letting our feelings take the lead can put us in that dangerous position of being led by the flesh instead of the Spirit. DM

Misusing "Church of Christ"

The following is an honest attempt at balance, and done, with God as my witness, out of love for God and the brethren. I am disturbed by divisive rhetoric, and while I know this has the potential to offend because I am calling out what I believe to be abuses, my effort is to work toward a better understanding and unity. I ask for patient consideration of what follows. The misuse of the phrase "Church of Christ" comes in at least two ends of the spectrum:

Misuse 1: using the phrase as an exclusive title and demanding that it alone will suffice.

This sees the phrase as a title to be used on everything, not just as a descriptive term. Thus there are "Church of Christ Preachers," "Church of Christ practices," and "Church of Christ doctrines." Those who use the phrase this way may believe that this is the only acceptable designation. If a congregation does not use "Church of Christ" on its sign, then it is ashamed of Christ and therefore not really His church. "I'm Church of Christ" is as significant as, "I'm a Christian." Even though there are other scriptural descriptions of the church, that doesn't matter. "Church of Christ" is the only name to use, and those who don't use it cannot be sound or are, at least, treading on dangerous ground and drifting. They believe that this is the only way to really identify a congregation that stands for the truth.

Misuse 2: using the phrase pejoratively as a label.

This second misuse is on the other end of the spectrum, perhaps even shunning the phrase altogether as a biblical idea. Sometimes it is used sarcastically or out of some level of scorn. We might hear negatively of "Church of Christ" (or "CoC") traditionalism, legalism, hypocrisy, or some other perceived problem. The "CoC" is depicted as a single conglomerate, and all who attend a "Church of Christ" fall under the judgment as being those who try to issue mandates where God has not. Some denigrate the perceived "CoC" method of interpretation (CENI = command, example, necessary inference), and speak as if all "CoC-ers" just want to restrict God's people and force them to be part of their denomination. Sometimes those who speak this way have themselves been wronged or hurt by a congregation or by those who attend a "Church of Christ." Some have grown up with the hypocrisy and are now very critical of "CoC" arguments or practices. Accordingly, there is, therefore, something inherently flawed about "the Church of Christ."

Why are both misuses a problem? Because both fall prey to speaking of that which is neither biblical nor real.

Regarding Misuse 1: there is no exclusive title given in the Bible for the church. There are several descriptions that are all perfectly acceptable, but no titles. Yes, the church does belong to Christ, but to insist that "Church of Christ" must be on every sign and must be the terminology used is to press what the Bible never presses and betrays a denominational and institutionalized concept of the body of Christ. Scripture, for example, speaks of the "church of God which is at Corinth" (1 Cor 1:2), the "church of the Thessalonians" (1 Thess 1:1), the "church of the firstborn who are enrolled in heaven" (Heb 12:23), "churches of Christ" (Rom 16:16), and so on. The only time "church of Christ" is used is in the plural, and it was simply describing more than one congregation that was sending greetings. There is nothing wrong with the phrase, but it is never used exclusively or denominationally. To choose an option found in Scripture is not being ashamed of Christ or the church, but is still falling under biblical authority and acceptable biblical practice. Therefore, to condemn a congregation for not going by that exclusive title (Church of Christ) is to go beyond Scripture (ironically) and assume a position of judgment God has not given.

Sadly, this very problem can help give rise to misuse 2.

Solution: use the full range of biblical terminology, and insist only on being a Christian according to Scripture. Don't make titles out of descriptions. Avoid denominational rhetoric that comes from exclusive naming. Go to the Scriptures and make sure that whatever traditions, practices, or terminology being used truly is biblical and not based upon mere preference or man-made tradition. It is one thing to insist on truth as found in Scripture; it is another to insist on an exclusive title that is never given as such in Scripture.

Regarding Misuse 2: this misuse can arise due to a faulty view of the church and poor terminology. Yet, the reaction can also betray other misconceptions and leave faulty impressions. The problem here is overgeneralization. With one swipe some will knock out just about anyone and everyone who has ever been a part of a "Church of Christ." To critically say that "the Church of Christ teaches…" is to imply that there is a single, unified teaching that comes from the institution known as the "Church of Christ." There is not. But, when the critique is made, what exactly is meant by "the CoC" or "the Church of Christ"? Is there some universal earthly institution so called being referenced? Who runs it and who belongs to it? Who decides the doctrine? Are they critiquing one congregation, many, or all? Are they opposing a few Christians or all Christians who attend a congregation with such on the sign of the building? Are they speaking of those involved in papers or colleges? Just calling out "the CoC" is a failure to work at making proper distinctions between universal and local, assembled or not. It further fails to distinguish between differing attitudes among Christians. As such, it is too vague to be helpful. Instead, this misuse oversimplifies, mischaracterizes, and caricatures the church without fairly representing the many who have avoided much of what is being criticized.

Solution: avoid sweeping generalizations and pejorative sarcasm. If an attitude or practice needs to be critiqued, then kindly refer to the "some" who need the attention without indicting everyone else who attends a group featuring a "church of Christ" sign, for not every Christian thinks or acts the way that is being criticized, and not every building with such a sign houses a group that does everything identically. If speaking of "the Church of Christ," then be specific about whether a local church or the universal body is under examination because no other institution actually exists in reality that controls the "CoC." If "CoC" refers neither to a local congregation nor the universal body (according to Scripture), then it references something that does not biblically exist. The critique then has little credibility and fails to build any bridges. Otherwise, be more particular. "Some Christians teach" (particular) is very different from "the CoC teaches" (general).

Using "Church of Christ" either exclusively (misuse 1) or as a pejorative label (misuse 2) will foster division, not unity. Instead, all need to seek the unity that is found only in Christ, insisting upon Scripture as the standard and submitting to the Lordship of Jesus. "Love one another" needs to be heard loud and clear. Being true, biblical Christians is the goal. None of this is to say that one side should deny doctrine or that the other side should never critique unscriptural ideas. It is to say, however, that any critique, and any dogmatic stand, will be counter-productive when it is not truly biblical. Hold each other accountable to God and Scripture, and do it out of love for one another. The cross of our Lord can accept nothing less, for He died for all. May God bless us all as we strive to follow only the Lord Jesus.

One of the responses I get to this is kind of a "yeah, but" response —yeah, but there is a core set of beliefs, doctrines, etc. and so it is proper to speak of it as "CoC" doctrine and so forth. Perhaps I should clarify further that I'm dealing not just with what *is* done, but with what *ought* to be done. That is, we can keep the status quo and keep using the terminology wrongly (on both sides), or we can challenge the status quo and strive to clean up the way we talk (on both sides) about the church and strive for what ought to be done. Yes, people do speak in these terms, and yes we might know what is meant. Yet it only furthers the misconceptions and resistance to what should be done in keeping biblical categories and terminology. I'm challenging both sides on this to refuse to capitulate to what *is* being done in order to foster what *should* be done.

It's Not Just a "Church of Christ" Thing

We hear various discussions about a variety of doctrines and practices in which someone will make a statement to the effect that some issue or practice is some peculiar "Church of Christ" thing. Besides the misuse of the phrase that continues to persist from many sources, often when someone does this it betrays a misunderstanding of the historical issues involved. For example, even though *a cappella* singing (i.e., without the instruments) has a centuries long, historical basis, and even though there are still other churches that do not use them (e.g., Orthodox), it is still supposedly just a "Church of Christ" (whatever is meant by that) thing. Never mind that many churches who call themselves "Church of Christ" actually use them. Occasionally I have seen some issue referenced that is supposedly some kind of "Church of Christ" doctrine based entirely in the Restoration Movement, yet it is easy to get the history wrong. Charges can easily be made without doing the homework, and it does a terrible injustice to all involved.

Add to this the continual referencing of ideas like the "Church of Christ" having unwritten creeds or not allowing dissent. The misrepresentations can abound. If no dissent is allowed, and we are all marching to the beat of the same drum in some robotic-like fashion, perhaps someone can explain why there are so many issues over which there are disagreements. For example, we see many attitudes and differences over matters like: Lord's Supper issues; Elder and deacon qualifications; The War question; The covering; Indwelling of the Holy Spirit; Bible classes; Women's roles; Limits of Romans 14; Divorce and remarriage particulars; Grace and works issues; Modesty issues; KJV-only… The list goes on, and it hardly indicates some kind of absolute conformity due to an unwritten creed enforced by…well, I have no idea who it would be enforced by. Perhaps some would try, but that's never worked very well for anyone involved.

The point is that brethren differ on many matters, and that is not characteristic of some unwritten creed mentality wherein everyone must agree on everything. It is far more indicative of allowing people to study out issues and come to their own conclusions. Are there going to be issues upon which most, if not all, will agree as decisions about fellowship are made? Of course, but, and this is very important, that is not just a "Church of Christ" thing. Every fellowship of every stripe does the very same thing — they just put the line at the different places, and that goes for the ones who complain about the "Church of Christ" as much as anyone. They have their lines, too.

Yes, people abuse and misuse the phrase in ways Scripture never does (which is why I keep putting it in quotes). To be sure, there are those who may seek to cause everyone to conform on virtually everything, but that's not just a "Church of Christ" thing. There are going to be traditionalists (good and bad), but that is not just a "Church of Christ" thing. There are going to be hard-nosed, stubborn people who refuse to allow disagreement, but that it not just a "Church of Christ" thing. There are going to be hypocrites, abusers of the text, unloving, unkind, and divisive people, but that is not just a "Church of Christ" thing. There are going to be phrases, ideas, and practices held in common, but that's not just a "Church of Christ" thing (I recently heard an evangelical say a prayer that sounded quite familiar in its phraseology). There will be those who have seen the abuses and hypocrisy, then feel the doctrine has been unfairly forced on them, but that is not just a "Church of Christ" thing. Name the problem. Name the attitude. It's not going to be just a "Church of Christ" thing, and when all is said and done, none of this in itself proves anything relative to truth (other than that some are inconsistent with it). Why, then, push this, as it serves to poison the well of legitimate discussion? Say "Church of Christ" or "Restoration Movement" in response to a position, and the argument is over, right? How does that help anyone who is searching for truth?

None of this is to say that we shouldn't try to find agreement. However, this needs to happen by finding common ground in the same foundation of authority. Here's a suggestion. If you want to challenge a doctrine or an argument, don't just reference some "Church of Christ" attitude or position. Such a generalization will not be helpful. Why not, instead, just go to Scripture and engage the arguments therein? Keep people accountable to God's word (2 Tim. 3:16-17). That will be far more helpful to everyone, and it will stress the fact that Scripture is authoritative. In the end, what churches practice in and of itself is not authoritative; the real question is whether or not they are conforming to the standard that is authoritative.

How do we know the thoughts of God?

Isaiah (55:3-11) says, "Listen..." To what? God has provided something that will "bear fruit and sprout" as it accomplishes what He desires. Isaiah tells us that this is God's word: "So will My word be which goes forth from My mouth; it will not return to Me empty, without accomplishing what I desire, and without succeeding in the matter for which I sent it." The power of the word of God is that it expresses the mind of God. To know God's thoughts and plans, we must know God's word. Guessing at it will never suffice as knowledge.

Paul also connects God's thoughts with God's word (1 Cor. 2). The only way to know the thoughts of someone is for that person to tell us what he is thinking. So it is with God. We cannot know what God thinks unless He tells us. God's mind has been revealed through the Holy Spirit "so that we may know the things freely given to us by God" (1 Cor. 2:12). This is one reason why God's silence is significant. Since we cannot quote an author on what he never said, we cannot infer God's approval for what He has not revealed, nor may we substitute our authority for His.

God's thoughts and ways will always be sovereign over our thoughts and ways. If we are going to appreciate God's grace and mercy, we must also appreciate the power that He has to offer these great blessings to us, and we must appreciate His word which informs us of His thoughts and plans.

God be thanked for His great power and His willingness to share His mind with us! DM

"CENI" Matters

CENI is the acronym usually given for "Command, Example, and Necessary Inference." Someone has suggested that we can just rearrange and call it NICE. The terminology has come under much scrutiny, and sometimes we must address these issues. Following are a few points to address some of the concerns.

First, we need to get past constant criticism of CENI. CENI is sometimes spoken of pejoratively, with the indication that it is a failed hermeneutic (method of interpretation). The problem may be that we have clouded the terminology so much that we have forgotten what basic communication is all about. CENI is an outgrowth of the basic principles of communication—what we use anywhere at any time for everyone.

As has been addressed, when we want to make our will known, how do we do it? Everyone who communicates in some fashion will do so by one of these three ways: 1) We tell someone; 2) We show someone; 3) We imply something we expect people to get. This is the more basic version of CENI. When people disparage CENI, they may not have thought this point through. Attacking CENI, as if that is inherently the problem, is attacking the foundation of communication, and it won't logically stand.

Here's the kicker: the whole principle of communication ("tell, show, and imply") is self-evident. Anyone who wants to deny this is free to try it, but they will be unable to deny it without telling, showing, or implying something about their own disagreement. To do so would be self-defeating, and we've been making this point.

What this means is that "tell, show, and imply" is a logically necessary process if any communication will take place. Again, it is the way we communicate anything. Now I realize that this doesn't get to the nuts and bolts of application, but I do think we need to get past the constant criticism of CENI because the principle that underlies it is logically necessary. The mistake, perhaps, has been that we haven't explained the fundamental communication process very well — we've left people wondering, "where do you find that in the Bible?" We find it anytime someone communicates anything, including in the Bible. It is a fundamental starting point, and I don't believe anyone can logically deny it without defeating their own denial.

CENI as a Hermeneutic?

Some may look at the above and think, "But that's still not really what we're objecting to. We are objecting to the idea that CENI is the be all and end all of interpretation." If objectors are wanting to talk about abuses, then they should address the specific abuses. There is no abuse simply in identifying the way that God communicates His will.

Is CENI or TSI (tell, show, and imply) a hermeneutical method? Again, we sometimes see the criticism of this as a failed hermeneutic (method of interpretation), but this misses the point of it. Let's elaborate.

Once again, TSI is foundational to any form of communication. There is no communication without it. It is inherent in any spoken or written communication (not just in studying the Bible). It is not, in itself, a hermeneutic or method of interpreting, but is rather foundational to any hermeneutic. That is, any hermeneutic will already assume the reality of TSI.

Hermeneutics is the science of interpretation. It is what we as the recipients (readers, hearers) bring to the communication process. TSI, on the other hand, is inherent in what the communicator gives.

That is, we, the readers or listeners, do not provide the TSI; we take the TSI that is given to us and try to understand what that means. TSI, then, is not a method of interpretation; it is the material that we try to interpret. We might misinterpret it. We might fail to get out of it what is intended. Nevertheless, it is the raw material that we use in order to try to understand what the author or speaker intends. There is no getting around this. No one interprets anything that is not first told, shown, or implied in some way.

We are speaking of the bare bones of what we work with when we do interpret. Instead of criticizing the communication process, let's recognize it for what it is and then deal with how we should properly understand the statements, examples, and implications.

Does CENI Come from God or Man?

We are challenging the idea that CENI is just a man-made hermeneutic on two grounds:

1. It is the formal, specific expression of how all communication works.

2. Because it is foundational to all communication, it is not really a hermeneutic; it is rather the material that is interpreted. Without something being told or shown, for example, what exactly is there to interpret? One might argue that inferring something is interpretation, and this is true. Yet inferring is done by the hearer or reader; the communicator implies, and this has to happen before anything can be logically inferred. Even so, our interpretation often builds on what has already been inferred (whether some inferences are justified is another discussion). Much interpretation is grounded on accepted assumptions and inferences.

Some still may think that all of this is just the product of human reason, and therefore is suspect as a binding principle. Let's consider this for a moment.

1. While human reason alone can be filled with problems (logical fallacies abound), we need to remember that God is the one who gave us the ability to reason. If human reason is never to be trusted, then what are we saying about the God who so equipped us? Just because some human reasoning is flawed does not therefore mean we cannot trust any human reasoning. That, too, would be fallacious reasoning, for the very argument that concludes human reason can never be trusted would have itself been reached by flawed human reasoning, and therefore should not be trusted as a conclusion.

2. Some principles are so fundamental to the process of reason, logic, and communication, that to deny them is self-contradictory. For example, what is often termed the "law of non-contradiction" recognizes that anything cannot be both what it is and what it isn't at the very same time and sense. This would be logically contradictory. It's also just plain common sense. The point we are making about "Tell, show, and imply," or the more formal CENI, is that these are so fundamental to the communication process that to deny them is self-defeating. Most people just take them for granted and do not need to spell them out. The reason we are spelling them out is because of the continual debates over CENI, many of which, in my judgment, seem to miss this fundamental point.

3. Since self-contradiction does not come from God, then we should recognize that anything that is logically self-evident (and thus cannot be denied without being self-contradictory) does, in fact, come from God, who is the epitome of all logic and reason. Not everything is self-evident, of course, and this is why we make arguments and offer further proofs. Something that is self-evident is true in itself; it needs no further justification because of how basic it is.

4. Since it is logically self-evident that communication involves some form of telling, showing, or implying (which may be derived through what is told or shown), then this process comes from God. It needs no further proof.

5. Scripture itself, which is God's communication, is given through the same process of communication. God tells (through direct statements and commands), God shows (through both positive and negative examples), and God implies (by leading us to conclude the truth of various principles). This cannot be reasonably denied. Every page of Scripture verifies this.

Will people differ over the applications that may come from this? Yes. But at least we should be agreeing on the fundamental communication process—a process that is rooted in the divine.

Tell, Show, and Imply: A Process or a System?

Let's sum up for a moment what we've been saying. Communication is a process, not a system. When we speak of telling, showing, and implying, we are speaking of a process—the same process for all communication. God has communicated to us through this very process. He has told us, shown us, and implied things for us that He expects us to get. For example, He has told us to love one another. He has shown us love in action through Jesus and His disciples. He has implied that this is a love that crosses boundaries of time and culture. In other words, we infer that His command to His disciples should go beyond just those original disciples and applies to people living now. We have gone from then and there to here and now by inference. How else can it be done?

In the context of talking about the process, CENI sometimes gets brought up as a form of abuse. The problem is that CENI is thought of as a system rather than a process. Even then, what is thought of as the system of CENI is really more about two primary concerns:

1. **Legalism.*** The idea is that we take commands coldly and think that we are earning salvation somehow. We take examples and make laws out of them. This turns our religion into some legalistic system that ignores grace for the most part. This lends itself to mere religious ritualism, while we demand that people conform to our alleged self-imposed code.

This is an important concern. The prophets often called out religious ritualism (e.g., see Isaiah 1), and we would be foolish to think it doesn't happen or cannot happen to us today. We should not take the process of communication and turn it into some cold system of law and judgment by which we just bash people into conformity and go through mere outward motion. If this is what CENI stands for, then surely we should all oppose the system. However, if we understand it as a process instead of a system, we can avoid this abuse.

2. **Abuses of Inference**. The idea here is that we make many inferences that are not necessary, then turn them into cold laws, demanding conformity on matters of judgment.

This is also an important criticism. For example, to expand upon a previous essay, we might take the name "Church of Christ." The phrase "churches of Christ" is used once, in Romans 16:16. We might reason thusly: the church is Christ's church; Paul refers to "churches of Christ"; singularly, it is "church of Christ." Therefore, churches should be called "The Church of Christ." Then, using this type of reasoning, any church that doesn't have "Church of Christ" on its sign is considered suspect at best, and lost at worst, being ashamed of the name of Christ. Then, we refer to ourselves as "Church of Christ" this or that (using it as an adjective). Surely we can see this type of reasoning is flawed, especially given that God's people are referred to in a number of different ways (including "church of God," "body," "kingdom," "church of the firstborn ones," etc.).** Demanding conformity on a name, used as a title, when Scripture does not do anything close to this, is bad inference turned into law. Yes, this does happen, and yes, it is an abuse of inference. It would also be a bad inference to infer, from what was just said, that I think it's okay to call ourselves anything we want or accept any possible name. I believe in honoring the Lord in how we refer to ourselves, but I don't believe in making laws the Lord didn't make.

While these criticisms can be well-founded, they do not negate the process of communication to which we all still appeal. We must not, as the adage goes, "throw the baby out with the bathwater." Our goal should not be to systematize a process. Rather, we should recognize the process for what it is, then seek to understand the information that appropriately flows from it. Remember, what is told, shown, or implied is not itself a method of interpretation (a hermeneutic). It is, rather, the raw material that we must look at in order to interpret. We take what is told, we consider what is shown, and we try to properly infer from what this information gives us. Yet, infer we must. To go from then and there to here and now can only come through inference. Instead of trying to fight the process, we should seek to understand better how to use the provided information as God intended.

* In my view, "legalism" as a term is too vague, and usually unhelpful. I use it here only because it is the term that I see so often brought up in discussions about these issues.

** "Church," of course, is often disputed because of its modern connotations. The *ekklesia* refers to an assembly or group, not some institutionalized concept, but that is the subject of another essay.

Honor your Father and Mother

"Honor your father and mother" is the fifth of the Ten Commandments (Exod. 20:12). The placement within the decalogue is not accidental, for this is the "hinge command" that affects both the previous four and the latter five. In the home is where children first learn about God and how to respect and revere Him, and the home is where they first learn about respect for others. If children do not first learn about God's authority and preeminence in the home, then where will they learn it, and what will they learn about it?

The first command is, "You shall have no other gods before Me" (Exod. 20:3). In the New Testament we are taught to "seek first His kingdom and His righteousness" (Matt. 6:33) and to avoid all forms of idolatry (Rom. 1:21-23). To say that God comes first is to recognize His rightful priority as the Creator and Ruler of all. If we do this, then we are recognizing that He maintains all authority and we must listen to Him.

Our respect for God is not based on whether or not we think God has adequately explained Himself to us. He is not amenable to us. As a parent has the right to tell a child what to do without the child fussing back, so God has the right to tell us what to do without our fighting back. Our place is to honor Him. We have no right to disobey Him just because we think He has given a command that doesn't make enough sense to our finite reason. Faith is trust, and if we trust God as the ultimate authority, then we will trust that all He tells us and shows us will be what we need. Learning this kind of trust begins in the home, when we first trust our parents. DM

On the Authority of Creeds 10

Apostasy has always been an ugly monster hovering over the household of God. Paul warned about it often (1 Tim. 4:1-5). Because of this, it is tempting for Christians to write up a list of positions on an issue or issues, publish it in some way, then hold it up as a standard for judgment on others. Those who do not hold to the published position are cut off and marked.

The history of "Christendom" has been marked by the appearance of creeds (e.g., The Apostles' Creed, the Nicene Creed, and the Athanasian Creed being the most prominent from early centuries). The word creed is from the Latin *credo*, meaning, "I believe." There is nothing wrong with stating a belief. This is necessary if we will take a stand for truth. One might even agree with the teaching of a creed; but a creed, as we are now speaking of it, goes beyond this (whether written or unwritten). It is essentially an authoritative statement, separate from Scripture, of a particular position (or positions) to which others are expected to assent. This goes beyond stating beliefs and is itself considered authoritative, taking on a life of its own. The problem is more associated with how people look to creeds as a standard to which others must submit.

The intent of a creed is to express essential biblical truth into which all must place their trust. They were usually written in times when error needed to be exposed, and so they served to warn of dangers. Those who wrote creeds were not just attempting to write their opinions. They believed they were teaching essential truth. We all do this, and, to be clear, we can learn from the ancient creeds. When they stated the truth, and especially in an understandable way, then they can be valuable, just as any article or statement by someone today. What, then, is the problem? Are we making a creed every time we write an article? Are we making a creed when we oppose error? Are we opposing creeds without any real solid reason for it? What is the real problem with creeds as they have come to be understood? Following are some of the reasons why we need to consider how authoritative a creed might actually be, and how a creed can go beyond stating beliefs to morph into an authoritative standard.

First, a creed is not comprised simply of articles of truth, but is given for the purpose of safeguarding a fellowship of something greater than any local church. In other words, they stake out the boundaries of fellowship on a broad, universal, scale. While they are intended to expose error, they draw the lines of fellowship for a brotherhood of believers. Framers of such a document are not content with allowing local congregations to deal with matters on their own. A creed crosses the local church lines with an implication that any churches or individuals who do not assent to the sentiments (if not the exact wording) of the document are to be considered dangerous and unworthy of fellowship. There is a difference between teaching truth and "letting the chips fall where they may," and trying to force the falling of the chips. Fellowship, which is a local and individual issue, will take care of itself for the most part. On the broad scale, fellowship is in the hands of God. A creed would attempt to remove it from God's hands and issue a decree on that broad scale. "With the development of heretical teaching, however, there was a natural tendency to use the creeds as a test of catholic orthodoxy" (Baker's Dictionary 147). The word "catholic" here means "universal." Creed-makers will not say that they are trying to force lines of fellowship or issue orthodoxy for a universal brotherhood, but this is exactly the effect.

Second, the creed is superimposed on Scripture. It is the formation of a succinct statement of truth, and becomes a sort of standard by which soundness will be measured for all. As long as one lines up to the view expressed in the creed (whether in the form of statements or questions), he is acceptable. Creed-makers do not act in accordance with the idea that the Bible is clear enough on the boundaries of fellowship; they need a statement telling everyone else where those boundaries are. Whether intentionally or not, they are creating and employing something beyond the Scriptures to measure soundness throughout the brotherhood of believers. A creed will almost always contain something either more or less than the Bible itself. Creed-makers will not say that they are trying to superimpose something on the Bible, but this is exactly the effect of the creed.

Third, the creed assumes a position of authority that is unwarranted. A creed is "authoritative," but only from a human viewpoint. Yet, what group or council of men has a right to declare anything for anyone else but themselves? What gives any group of men on a broad scale (whether it is through a paper, college, or any other organized effort) a right to issue a statement to which they expect others to assent on the threat of disfellowship? Concerning creeds, Alexander Campbell, in his debate against N.L. Rice, argued, "They are called human, not merely because they are the production of human effort, but because they are also the offspring of human authority. No one can, in reason and truth, assign to them a divine authority; because no man can produce any precept or divine warrant for their manufacture. No apostle, prophet, or evangelist gave any authority to any church, community, or council, to furnish such a document" (763).

Fourth, a creed is an instrument of division, not unity. While the creed is a result of an organized attempt to unite, the reality is that it serves as a catalyst for broad-based divisions. Were it not for a creed, there would be more likelihood of local congregations handling their problems regarding fellowship independently, but a creed stirs up an unrest on a broad scale, and so has a large impact on many congregations. Now the tone becomes "line up and divide," contributing to suspicion and division. They further the party, sectarian spirit. Alexander Campbell affirmed the following proposition in his debate with Rice: "Human Creeds, as Bonds of Union and Communion, are necessarily Heretical and Schismatical." Creeds will divide, not unite.

Fifth, the historical tendency was to continue elaboration. It became "difficult to stop the process of elaboration, and the continuing requirement of this or that new dogma on pain of eternal damnation could only enhance the power of the church, weaken true faith and its confession, and call forth from protesting or reforming groups opposing statements which had also to be given some measure of symbolic significance" (Baker's Dictionary 148). Any given issue has a plethora of attached issues with it. Some will agree to disagree on the peripheral points as long they agree on the central point (even though the peripheral points may have serious consequences themselves). At some point many will feel it necessary to elaborate and narrow down the qualifications for acceptableness. That process becomes never-ending and self-defeating.

Sixth, a creed is often the result of over-reacting and over-reaching. Let there be no mistake: Christians ought to oppose error (cf. Titus 1:13). However, creeds were the result of going too far the other direction by attempting to enforce orthodoxy on a brotherhood of believers. This, too, is error. David Bercot, in his book *Will the Real Heretics Please Stand Up*, wrote, "For every heretic who moves away from true doctrine in one direction, there is a well-meaning 'defender of the faith' who tried to defend orthodoxy by going to an equal and opposite extreme. Unfortunately, the 'defender of the faith' often pulls much of the church with him in his over-reaction. The end result is that the heretic succeeds in adulterating the church, but in the opposite way from what he started out" (133). By a sublime attempt to activate a universal brotherhood, the supporters of a creed go into another kind of error.

Seventh, the nature of a creed is that it stifles Bible study. By implementing a "do this or else" mentality, a creed will strangle any attempts to further study the particular issues involved. The creed makes it so that "this is the final answer, no ifs, ands, or buts," and any suggestions or questions to the contrary (even from meaningful Christians attempting to study something out for themselves) is automatically put into the category of efforts to compromise truth. While Christians ought not to compromise truth (Prov. 23:23), neither should they squelch honest attempts to study, even if such study must delve into differing positions. Fellowship will then take care of itself on the local level. I must oppose anything that would effectively end open study.

I have tried to make it clear that the issue I have with creeds is not opposition to error, nor simply the statement of beliefs. I might agree with the basic sentiments expressed in a creed (e.g., the Deity of Christ), but the issue with a creed is that it oversteps the line of teaching and moves into the realm of authoritative boundary-marking for a group of believers larger than a local congregation. This is without authority altogether, and steps upon the hands of God, who alone has universal authority.

How can we avoid this problem?

1. Let local churches handle their own issues of fellowship. I will try to just teach what I believe to be the truth, and let the chips fall where they may.

2. Avoid a "do this or else" mentality when it comes to various issues. This effectively squelches Bible study, and Christians have no right to issue universal dictums or ultimatums.

3. Take a balanced approach to the issues to be faced. I do not encourage one to be weak in dealing with error, but "jumping the fence" to another extreme is not justified either.

4. Be committed to your own local situation. Do not be so concerned about what is going on throughout the brotherhood. Concentrate on working where you are, and take advantage of opportunities to teach when you can.

A creed is a sectarian trap. If not careful, however, Christians may fall prey to the allurement of a universally line-drawing document (or even verbal understanding) that carries the weight of a council of men whom they respect. Instead, constant reaffirmation of the all-sufficiency of Scripture is needed. May God help us fight error, but may He also help us to fight it without going too far the other direction. A creed does just that.

On the Failure of Creeds

We end this essay with some pertinent points made by the preacher Benjamin Franklin (not the one most will think of, but a gospel preacher of that same name in the 19th century). The following is an excerpt from "The Infallibly Safe Course," *New Testament Christianity*, ed. by Z.T. Sweeney:

"But there are so many creeds, all claiming to be right, that I should not know which to take. They were all made by learned men, and if they can not agree on the kind of a creed, how am I to decide which is right?" says one. It is a matter of great moment and of much relief that, aside from all these conflicting, clashing, and erring creeds, there is one book that all parties concede is right. They all agree that the Bible is right — that it came from God. They all further agree that it contains the law of God — that the law of the Lord is perfect. The only wonder is, that man ever attempted to make any other creed or law for the Church. Such an undertaking could not have commenced without two wicked assumptions:

1. That the law of God, as set forth in the Bible, is not sufficient — is a failure.

2. That the insufficiency or failure can be remedied by weak, erring, and uninspired men.

No man of intelligence will affirm, in plain terms, that the Bible is not sufficient for the government of the saints; or that man — uninspired man — can make a creed that will serve a better purpose than the Bible. Still such affirmations are implied in every attempt made by uninspired men to make a creed. If you admit, as all are bound to do, that the law of God is in the Bible; that nothing may be added to it, nothing taken from it, and that no part of it may be changed, there is not an excuse in the world for making another law. The law of God in the Bible is the law, the divine law, the supreme law, in the kingdom of God; and it is a treasonable movement to attempt to get up another constitution, law, name, body, or officers, apart from the constitution, law, name, body, and officers as found in the Bible.

But the matter now in hand is to find a safe course to pursue. Can this be done? All admit the Bible is right. All admit that the law of God in the Bible is right. All admit that those who follow the Bible honestly and faithfully, in faith and practice, will be saved. All admit that wherever any creed differs from the Bible is wrong. Then it is infallibly safe to take the Bible and follow it. When men undertake to prove that a human creed is a good one, they argue that it is like the Bible. If a creed like the Bible is a good one, why will not the Bible itself do? If the Bible will not serve the purpose — is insufficient and a failure — a creed like it would be equally insufficient. When men make a creed to do what the Bible would not do, they should certainly make it different from the Bible, or it would serve no better purpose than the Bible itself."

Discerning Good and Evil

Galatians 5:19-21 provides a list of sins that will keep one out of the kingdom of heaven, concluding with "things like these." How do we know what is "like these" unless we infer from the principles given? How can God expect us to figure that out without explicitly stating it? The only way to make sense of this is to consider the principles and infer what God expects us to get. There are "things like these" that can keep us out of heaven, so this must be vital for us to figure out, and we must learn to infer properly.

The Hebrews writer speaks of the mature, who "because of practice have their senses trained to discern good and evil" (5:12-14). Discernment is the ability to see a principle and make proper applications. To discern is to apply reason, to draw conclusions based upon the given information.

Mature people don't need everything spelled out in detail in order to understand. They can grasp a principle and make applications appropriately. They are able to draw the needed conclusions from the principles about what's right or wrong. To do it, however, requires drawing conclusions that are not explicitly stated. This is called inference.

Are inferences necessary for understanding God's will? If not, we will need a good explanation (based on inference, no less) for Galatians 5 and Hebrews 5, both of which require drawing conclusions about good and evil beyond what the text explicitly states. We may debate the particulars of the conclusions, but the principle here is firmly established, and the applications of these texts requires inferring from implications given through principles. DM

Fellowship and Division

We have considered a number of biblical principles concerning biblical authority and how it practically affects our work for God. Ideas have consequences; issues do not occur in a vacuum. People are affected by the specific issues that arise. The question is, how do we respond? What do we do when issues arise that would cause us to compromise biblical principles? What if our involvement in them would cause us to do something that we conscientiously believe to be wrong? Issues related to authority have an impact on fellowship. Here we consider some biblical principles dealing with fellowship in Christ and what happens when division occurs.

What Is Fellowship?

Generally, fellowship is an association or friendly relation. Broadly, we have "fellowship" in a mutual, friendly relationship. In this general sense, fellowship is not based on a spiritual relationship, but on being human. It is association with another human being rather than being "in Christ." This is not the same as biblical fellowship. Biblically, fellowship (*koinonia*) is a joint participation in activities related to being Christians. It is a communion, an association involving close, mutual relations due to having a common faith and salvation in Jesus.

We must be careful not to confuse biblical fellowship with general fellowship. Fellowship in Christ is an outgrowth of our relationship to God; general fellowship is an outgrowth of being human. Fellowship in Christ is more restricted than general fellowship. Jesus ate with sinners, but this did not imply that He thought they were in fellowship with God. Friendliness with others is not the same as endorsement of a spiritual relationship (see Matt. 9:10-13). Jesus even ate in the home of Pharisees (Luke 7:36).

Fellowship in Christ is not based upon just doing anything together. Socializing together is not what constitutes fellowship in Christ. As Christians, we will have social contact (e.g., eating together), but fellowship in Christ is based upon our spiritual relationship we have with God, and our common spiritual blessings we share in Christ. It is a deeper foundation than outward socializing. While outward association like eating together may characterize those who have fellowship, the fellowship itself is much deeper than that.

Fellowship is first based upon our relationship with God. Fellowship with God exists when we have a joint participation with Him, made possible when we submit to His will and, by His grace, our sins are forgiven. The purpose of the gospel is to bring sinners into fellowship with God (Eph. 2:1-22; Rom. 5:6-11; 1 John 1; 1 Cor. 1:9; 2 Thess. 2:14). Sin breaks fellowship and separates us from God (Isa. 59:1-2). Through the death of Christ, reconciliation is possible so that we may once again be in fellowship with God (2 Cor. 5:21).

Our first priority must be our relationship with God. We must not be more concerned about fellowship among men than we are about our fellowship with God. Fellowship among brethren will follow properly when we first have our relationship with God established.

Fellowship with God is a conditional relationship. We must be "in Christ," followers of His will, and not turning back and quitting (Eph. 1:3; Gal. 3:26-27; 1 John 1:7; Heb. 10:39). Fellowship with brethren is based upon what we share in common due to our relationship with God. For example, in Christ, we share:

1. A common faith (Titus 1:4; Eph. 4:5). Our faith stems from hearing the word of God (Rom. 10:17). For us to have a common faith, we must share the common standard. If people are holding to a different faith, then our basis for fellowship is lost.

2. A common salvation (Jude 3). Our salvation is based upon the reign and grace of God (see Isa. 52:7 again). We share in common the grace of our King who died for us. Yet this also requires that we teach the truth about salvation. When salvation is taught many different ways, how is there a basis for fellowship?

3. Unity. Our relationship should be characterized by unity, agreement, and harmony because we hold to the same Lord and the same standard (Phil. 2:1-5; Eph. 4:1-6; 1 Cor. 1:10). Disunity can cause unbelief (John 17:20-21). If we are concerned about loving God and loving others, then we will do all we can to live in peace with one another (Rom. 12:18; 1 Cor. 13). The fervent love for one another is characterized by those who have been born of God's word (1 Pet. 1:22-23). If our love is based on another standard, then it cannot be what God wants for us.

4. Joint participation in the work of God. This involves a sharing in the work that God has given His people (Eph. 2:10). We share in the spread of the gospel and in strengthening each other (Phil. 1:5; 4:15; Gal. 6:6). We share in providing help to needy saints (2 Cor. 8:3-4) and doing good for all (Gal. 6:6-10). We also share in worship and praise to our God (1 Cor. 10:16-17; Acts 2:42).

The fellowship that believers share in Christ is precious and not to be lightly regarded. Further, we need to be aware of two extremes what it comes to fellowship: 1) extending spiritual fellowship to those out of fellowship with God (1 Cor. 5:1-2), and 2) excluding from our fellowship those who are in fellowship with God (3 Jn. 9-10). Fellowship with others is subject to some judgment. Sometimes, due to circumstances, we may not make the right judgment. Therefore, we must be very careful to make sure we have the facts and the right standard (Scripture) to make proper judgments.

Fellowship Is An Individual Issue.

Fellowship is primarily determined individually (Gal. 2:9). Individuals must make sure they are right with God (2 Pet. 1:10). This does not mean that what the congregation does is of no importance, for individuals are affected by congregational action.

While congregations are judged in time (Rev. 2-3), individuals stand before God in final judgment (Rom. 14:12; 2 Cor. 5:10). It is even possible for a congregation to have problems while some individuals within that group are right with God (Rev. 2:18-29; 3:1-6). Yet just because we are part of a congregation that is doing what is right does not mean our names are enrolled in heaven.

Fellowship is determined within each autonomous congregation. Universally, the church is made up of individuals, not sub-groups. Congregations are not structurally tied to each other in some interconnected web. As a group, we have no say as to who or what another congregation has fellowship with. That is not ours to determine. We can only have a say among ourselves as to whom we accept into our fellowship (see Acts 9:26-28).

Congregations are autonomous. There is no universal format (aside from Scripture) that determines with whom we may have fellowship. No universal body makes that decision for us. Our primary concern, then, is not with "brotherhood fellowship." Some seem to be quite concerned about universal, brotherhood fellowship. Who is in fellowship with whom? No Christian or organization, however, has any say about who is in fellowship with whom on any universal basis. We determine fellowship as someone comes into contact with our group. Another who lives thousands of miles away is not in fellowship with us locally, unless we choose to participate in supporting him in preaching. Whether or not he is in fellowship with God is up to God to determine. Our arena of fellowship concerns what touches us individually and locally.

The late Robert Turner made the following helpful comments about this issue:

"As we individually obey the gospel we pledge ourselves to serve God. To Him we must individually give account when life is through (Matthew 16:24; Romans 14:4, 12). Following this agreement of allegiance, and subject to this obligation, we join hands with others to work and worship together in a local fellowship, or congregation. God commands this union; the ties of this association are grand and its obligations are real; but it remains the means of serving the Master, and must never become our Master.

Fellowship of men with men is an earthly tie which has an acceptable religious significance only when it complements our service to God. It is given divine regulations, but men do not always follow those regulations. One who counts on the outward bond of church fellowship alone to guarantee his spiritual redemption, leans on a broken reed. No, I do not depreciate the importance of the church. I seek to emphasize the meaning of the true church, as God's people, who do God's work in God's way — praised for their allegiance and service to God, rather than for their faithfulness to the party.

Brethren who are primarily interested in keeping their fellowship with God intact, will be drawn to one another by his common interest, and find a congregational fellowship that forecasts the sweetness of heaven." (Two "Fellowships")

What Happens When We Disagree?

Judgments must be made concerning the extent and effect of disagreements. While this is sometimes difficult to determine due to a host of issues, here are some questions and suggestions we might think about:

Does the fellowship cause us to engage in sin? If so, then we should not have fellowship (cf. Eph. 5:11). Some matters, of course, are clearly spelled out as sinful and our only option is to refuse fellowship. If one is engaged in fornication or is a liar, for example, then we do have clear instructions about this type of behavior (cf. 1 Cor. 5:11; 6:9-10; Gal. 5:19-21; Rom. 1).

Does the issue affect the local group? Do we respect the local congregation and its independence? Is the issue based upon an individual's conscientious decisions? If pushed, how will the issue affect the group? Will it cause others to violate their consciences? Have we properly studied and applied the teachings of Romans 14? The point is that we have to carefully consider where exactly the issue over which we differ fits. The first reaction should never be to divide. We should always, out of love, seek to be united first. We should always respect others' consciences. We should be willing to study together and strive to come to a common mind.

Some issues most certainly will affect the entire group. If one is determined to bring in instruments of music into the assembly for worship, for example, then everyone present will be affected. The way a congregation spends its money and resources will affect the entire group because of the nature of collected funds.

Other issues are much more individual in nature. For example, the extent to which a family will participate in various holidays is individually determined. What another practices on this does not necessarily involve us or the entire group. Therefore, there may be no need to break fellowship (cf. Rom. 14). This will take hard work, much love, and great patience. If we broke fellowship over every difference, there would be no congregation.

When people practice activities that others cannot, through faith, engage in, and these practices are pushed upon the group, then fellowship will be broken. There can be no joint participation. Those who are concerned about the unity of the Spirit and with the consciences of others will not try to push unnecessary activities upon the group that they know others cannot accept by faith. This is especially true when these practices are admittedly non-essential. Why would brothers concerned with unity do this? Even if they think they have "rights," what kind of attitude pushes such issues to the point of division (cf. 1 Cor. 8:8-13)? We must respect our brethren for whom Christ died more than our perceived rights.

We desire unity, but we cannot violate our biblically trained consciences to participate in things that are wrong. However, fellowship is not based upon robotically agreeing upon every single point of issue. We need to be careful to maintain fellowship based upon Scripture, not upon our own opinions.

Apostasy and Division Result From A Lack of Respect for Authority.

We have considered many facets of authority. Most of what has been studied has been fairly basic. Yet if it is that simple, then why are people divided? Why do divisions occur, and what can be done about it? Here is what we wish to stress here: division is very much connected to problems over authority. One might respond that divisions occur more because of bad attitudes, but even bad attitudes are a manifestation of a failure to submit to the authority of the King.

What is apostasy? The idea is "falling away" due to rebellion: "to cause people to rebel against or to reject authority — 'to incite to revolt, to cause to rebel.'" (Louw and Nida 498). Note that apostasy is a rejection of authority.

Apostasy is foretold by Paul (1 Tim. 4:1-5; 2 Thess. 2:3-12). The term used in 1 Timothy 4:1 coincides with the above definition.

There would be a rebellion against the authority of God. This would include forbidding marriage and certain foods (vv. 2-5). Yes, even forbidding something that God allows is a way to reject His authority. It's not just about doing what He doesn't want; it's also about not allowing what He does. Either way, His authority is being rejected. The related term in 2 Thessalonians 2:3-12 means, "to rise up in open defiance of authority, with the presumed intention to overthrow it or to act in complete opposition to its demands." (Louw and Nida 497).

We are told that some would reject authority and act in complete defiance against it. Though many who reject authority do not think they intend to defy God, the results are the same. Because some would not love the truth, God would allow them to be deceived. A similar warning is given in 2 Timothy 4:2-4. There would be those who accumulate their own teachers to tell them what they want to hear. The point is that there is a marked rejection of God's authority and an increased desire to hear what popular crowd-pleasers will say.

Apostasy, then, comes from disrespecting God's authority. The apostasy of 2 Thessalonians 2 is lawlessness (vv. 7-8). There are those who will lead others down this path of lawlessness. Leaders of movements will "cause people to rebel or to reject authority," causing a falling away. Even those who start with good intentions can lead others down the wrong path (Matt. 15:13-14). The result will be apostasy, even though they did not intend to depart from truth. Remember the judgment scene of Matthew 7:21-23.

When we begin to reject some of God's authority, we are headed down that road to apostasy. It usually begins a little at a time. Small compromises are made here and there, and these can lead to greater compromises. Generally, there is less stress put on what Scripture teaches, and more stress put upon what the leaders of a particular dogma say. Soon, their authority is accepted above that of the

Scriptures. What the leaders say, orally or in publications, is accepted above what the Bible says. This is why we need to constantly reassess our attitude and commitment to the truth of God's word. Is our commitment to God and what the word says, or is it some particular man, group, or dogma? (1 Thess. 2:13; Acts 17:11).

When apostasy occurs, there is sure to be division that takes place. Those who reject God's authority will necessarily break with those who refuse to go down that path (cf. 1 John 2:18-19). Those who incite others to reject authority are divisive persons who need to be marked (Rom. 16:17-18; Titus 3:9-11; Jude 8-11). These are men who will deceive others with smooth talk. They will pull others away from truth because they have their own agenda.

What Can Be Done?

1. A return to scriptural authority is needed.

This includes making sure that what we believe and practice has proper biblical warrant. We cannot provide authority for ourselves. We need to get back to Scripture and stress our need to listen to God and do what He says (Prov. 14:12; Col. 3:17). This also means we need to be teaching the need for authority. The kingship and authority of Jesus must be taught to every generation. If not, the next generation will take further steps away from God. Because of Israel's failure to teach succeeding generations the importance of what God said, "there arose another generation ... who did not know the Lord, nor yet the work which He had done for Israel" (Judges 2:10).

2. A return to proper attitudes is needed.

First, we need proper attitudes toward God and His expressed will in Scripture. This means that we must be committed to knowing and properly interpreting Scripture, doing what Scripture teaches, and diligently teaching others. This mirrors the concern of Ezra: "For Ezra had set his heart to study the Law of the Lord, and to do it and to teach his statutes and rules in Israel" (7:10).

Second, we need to maintain love, concern, and respect for others. We cannot "run roughshod" over others simply because we have a selfish desire to practice something. This will only lead to division. Love needs to be genuine, and we need to be devoted to one another, not pushing selfish agendas to the harm of brethren and churches (Rom. 12:9-18; Phil. 2:1-5).

3. A return to our mission is needed.

Our mission is primarily spiritual. While there are social benefits, we may easily get sidetracked with social and recreational issues. These, in turn, have caused much division. If we keep our focus upon the real nature of our work in glorifying God through the spread of the gospel, we minimize potential problems. "For the Son of Man came to seek and to save the lost" (Luke 19:10).

Therefore, lift up the crucified Christ (John 12:32; 1 Cor. 1:18-2:2). If we resort to other means to draw people in, then we have left our foundations. Let's be committed to emphasizing Christ and Him crucified. If the message of the cross is not enough, nothing else will be sufficient to save souls.

Conclusion

Authority is no light matter. We need to handle the Scriptures accurately and be committed to the truth. We are not the standard; God's word gives us the standard. If we are wrong, then we need a willingness to change and conform to what the Scriptures teach. We need open hearts and minds, ready to listen so that we will accept the principles found throughout the word of God.

Bibliography

Auerbach, David H. *Is Instrumental Music Permitted in Jewish Worship?* Jewish Perspectives. http://www.jewishperspectives.com/music.asp (accessed March 18, 2016).

Elwell, Walter A., ed. *Baker's Dictionary of Theology.* Grand Rapids, MI: Baker Books, 1996.

Baptist Confession of Faith of 1689, The. http://www.1689.com/confession.html (accessed March 18, 2016).

Bauer, Walter, Arndt, William, and Wilbur Gingrich. *A Greek-English Lexicon of the New Testament and Other Early Christian Literature.* Chicago: University of Chicago Press. pp. 277-278.

Bercot, David. *Will the Real Heretics Please Stand Up?* Amberson, PA: Scroll Publishing Company, 1989.

Calvin, John. *The Complete Biblical Commentary Collection of John Calvin.* Kindle edition.

Campbell-Rice Debate. https://archive.org/stream/campbellricedeba00campiala/campbellricedeba00campiala_djvu.txt (accessed March 18, 2016).

Encyclopaedia Britannica online: http://www.britannica.com (accessed March 18, 2016).

Kreeft, Peter. *Socratic Logic.* 3rd ed. South Bend, IN: St. Augustine Press, 2008.

Louw, Johannes P. and Eugene A. Nida, eds. *Greek-English Lexicon of the New Testament Based on Semantic Domains.* 2nd ed. New York: United Bible Societies, 1989.

Institution. Wikipedia. http://en.wikipedia.org/wiki/Institution#Institutionalization (accessed March 18, 2016).

Origen. *Commentary on the Gospel of John.*

Packer, J.I. *Fundamentalism and the Word of God.* Grand Rapids, MI: Eerdmans Publishing Co., 1958.

Price, John. *Old Light on New Worship.* Avinger, TX: Simpson Publishing Company, 2005.

Ramm, Bernard. *The Pattern of Authority.* Grand Rapids, MI: Eerdmans Publishing Co., 1957.

Sweeney, Z.T., ed. *The Infallibly Safe Course.* New Testament Christianity. Vol. 3, 1930.

Turner, Robert. Two "Fellowships." Plain Talk. Vol. 1, No. 11, November 1964.

Turner, Robert. *What Did God "Establish"?* Plain Talk. Vol. 1, No. 1, January 1964.

Made in the
USA
Middletown, DE